☆

CALIFORNIA

POLITICS

☆

CALIFORNIA PUBLICATIONS IN POLITICAL SCIENCE

Editor: John, Editor

CHANDLER PUBLICATIONS IN POLITICAL SCIENCE

Victor Jones, Editor

CALIFORNIA
POLITICS

FOURTH EDITION

☆

Joseph P. Harris
University of California, Berkeley

CHANDLER PUBLISHING COMPANY
124 Spear Street · San Francisco, California 94105

Science Research Associates, Inc.
259 East Erie Street, Chicago, Illinois 60611

A Subsidiary of IBM

Contents

☆

Preface   ix

1 · California's Political Profile   1

The Progressive Movement
The Republican Era
Upton Sinclair's EPIC Movement
A Democratic Interlude
The Warren Era
Democratic Victories
The 1962 State Election
The 1964 Primary and General Election
The 1966 Primary and General Election
Party Trends in Registration and Elections
Party Victories: Retrospect and Prospect
The Pattern of California Politics

2 · Political Party Organizations: Official and Unofficial   41

How a Political Party Qualifies
The State Convention

The State Central Committee
Members of the National Party Committee
County Central Committee
Other Party Committees
Unofficial Political Organizations
The California Republican Assembly
The California Democratic Council

3 • Nominations and Elections   55

Types of Elections
Qualifications for Voting
*Nomination of Candidates: Direct Primary
  Elections*
The Presidential Preference Primary
Campaign Strategy and Tactics
The High Cost of Political Campaigns
The Election of Judges
*The Politics of Nonpartisanship: County, City,
  and Other Local Elections*

4 • Lawmakers and Lawmaking   83

Pressure Groups
The Press
The Politics of the Legislature
Legislative Apportionment
The Initiative and Referendum
The Recall of Public Officers

5 • On Being Active in Politics   121

Suggested Readings on California Politics   125

Index   127

Illustrations

☆

Official Party Organization in California 42
California Congressional Districts, 1961 93
California State Assembly Districts, 1965 96
California State Senatorial Districts, 1965 97
Two Legislative Districts in Los Angeles County 111

Preface

☆

This short study is an introduction to politics in California. It is intended not only to provide the reader with the major facts about the political system of the state, which in many respects is unique, but also to explain the underlying forces and to summarize the most significant historical developments in the political life of the state. The intelligent citizen needs to know much more than the law, the procedure, and the bare facts about nominations, elections, campaigns, and political parties; he needs to understand how and why elections are won and lost, and the underlying forces and groups within the state which play a continuing role in the struggle for power and control of government and its policies.

Politics is the first business of the citizen, but a business which is too often neglected. The art of governance in a democracy depends upon citizen understanding and participation in politics, especially by a substantial number of opinion leaders. It is hoped that this short book will increase the understanding and appreciation of politics by the readers, and will encourage many to take a more active part in public affairs.

Many sections of the study have been completely rewritten in this edition to reflect recent political developments in the state. The historical background has been expanded substantially and new sections dealing with recent elections have been added. The section on legislative apportionment has been enlarged and brought up to date.

The author wishes to express his indebtedness to many former students at the University of California, Berkeley, whose interest, enthusiasm, and inquiring minds contributed much to the original study. It is a source of deep satisfaction to the author that many of them are today active participants in California politics.

J. P. H.

Berkeley, California
October 1, 1966

☆

CALIFORNIA

POLITICS

☆

chapter 1

California's Political Profile

☆

California has become the most populous state in the Union, a leading state in its economy, industrial development, agriculture, educational institutions, and in many other respects. Its state government is the largest in the country and has one of the finest state civil-service systems. The county, city, school-district, and other local governments are noted for their high standards of administration and rank among the best in the country.

California leads also in the difficult problems which face state and local governments. Almost every governmental problem which other states face is present in exaggerated form in California. These include its rapidly growing population, race relations, crime, urban blight, welfare, health, smog, traffic, transportation, education, recreation, and many others.

In this book we are concerned with the politics and political institutions of the state, the means whereby the citizens select their officers and control their government, and the ways in which political leaders provide the leadership that is so essential in modern society. No state or nation can cope with the varied, complex, and urgent problems of modern society without highly developed political institutions and able political leadership.

California has long been regarded as having unique political institutions. Several times in its history liberal or radical movements have arisen to challenge the old order, flourished, and then declined as rapidly as they arose, but not without leaving an imprint on the life of the state. A Workingman's party, formed in 1867, became a power in the state within a few years, electing its nominee to the Supreme Court in 1874. Despite the united opposition of the two major parties, which ran a combined slate of "nonpartisan" candidates, it elected one-third of the delegates to the Constitutional Convention of 1878–1879. Severely repressed by state and local authorities and forced in 1880 to hold its meetings secretly on sand lots, it nevertheless elected 10 senators and 16 assemblymen. Three years later it had disappeared. Greatly impressed by the rapid rise and fall of the Workingman's party, Lord Bryce wrote in his classic study of American government, *The American Commonwealth,* that the political situation in California was peculiar and dangerous.

California is noted for its fads, religious sects, and political extremism both of the right and the left. Upton Sinclair's "End Poverty in California" movement and the Townsend old-age-pension plan in the 1930s are examples of such movements which have risen, flourished briefly, and then disappeared. More recently and currently, the effort of the extreme right to take over the Republican party and the rise in 1966 of the "New Left" dedicated to ending the Viet Nam war are examples of extremism in politics.

THE PROGRESSIVE MOVEMENT

California has had many liberal and radical movements which have challenged the leadership of the two major political parties for a period until they disappeared or were absorbed within the ranks of one of the parties. The most important of these, which left a lasting mark on the politics of the state, was the Progressive movement of 1908–1918. The founders of the movement were two journalists, Chester Rowell of the *Fresno Republican* and

Edward A. Dickson of the *Los Angeles Express*. With adjoining desks in the press row of the state legislature in 1907, they witnessed the disgraceful spectacle of its control by political bosses who were the tools of the Southern Pacific Railroad, which virtually ran the state. In an editorial entitled "Adjourned, Thank God," Chester Rowell declared that "in shameless servility, blatant indecency, and total unfitness, this legislature stands at the very bottom of the long list of boss-ridden legislatures that have disgraced California." Demanding that the state follow the example of Wisconsin and overthrow corrupt corporation government, he concluded: "If we are fit to govern ourselves, this is the last time we will submit to being governed by the hired bosses of the Southern Pacific Railroad Company." [1] Most of the independent press of the state agreed with the editorial.

For many years the Southern Pacific Railroad Company virtually controlled the state government and its influence also extended to local governments. After merging with its competitors, it owned 85 percent of the railroad mileage of the state, as well as river and ocean shipping lines, ferries, and urban transportation systems. The state's largest landowner, it was a giant corporation overshadowing other business organizations. To protect its varied interests and to prevent effective regulation by the state, the Railroad maintained control over the state government, especially the legislature. William F. Herrin, its chief counsel, directed its political activities with a staff in Sacramento which was popularly known as the Southern Pacific Political Bureau. John R. Haynes, a leading reformer and opponent of the boss and machine rule that widely prevailed, wrote: "From the village constable to the governor of the state, . . . the final selection of the people's officials lay with Mr. Herrin or his subordinates in the railroad machine." [2]

The Southern Pacific's control over the state government and

---

[1] Quoted by George E. Mowry, in *The California Progressives* (Berkeley: University of California Press, 1951), p. 65. The following account draws heavily upon this work.

[2] Quoted in Mowry, p. 16.

some of the large cities was exercised largely through the dominant Republican party. In a period when nominations for public office were made by boss-controlled party nominating conventions, the Railroad controlled the conventions and was thus able to dictate who would be the party's nominees for governor, state officials, members of the legislature, judges, and local officers. It was thus able to control the actions of the state and local governments, especially in matters affecting its interests. Many newspapers were recipients of its bounty and its influence reached to all parts of the state. A similar control was exercised by the leading railroad in many other states during the latter half of the nineteenth century.

Public opposition to the political domination of the state by the Southern Pacific preceded the Progressive movement. As early as 1898 the Democratic candidate for governor attacked the Railroad and polled a respectable vote. The Democratic candidates for governor in 1902 and again in 1906 made the Railroad a central issue in the campaign and narrowly failed of election in a period when Republican candidates ordinarily carried the state by large majorities. Many Democratic office holders, however, were subservient to the Railroad, accepting its campaign contributions and other favors.

In the decade following 1900 the party machines in San Francisco and Los Angeles, which were closely allied with the Railroad, were discredited by the public exposure of widespread corruption, graft, and bribery. After several years of open warfare over the closed shop in San Francisco, organized labor in 1901 formed the Union Labor party and succeeded in electing its candidate for mayor. Abe Ruef, a Republican ward leader who had earlier failed in an attempt to seize control of the Republican machine, became the leader of the new Labor party, which swept into power in a surprising victory in 1905, defeating a coalition ticket of the Republican and Democratic machines. Under the direction of Ruef as the new city boss, the city government entered into a period of corruption, graft, bribery, and protection of the underworld which outdid the more circumspect corruption of the previous political machines. But the Ruef machine made one fatal mistake; it elected an honest man as prosecuting attorney, who worked with the outraged citizens to investigate and later to prosecute persons who were accused of accepting or giving bribes.

In one of the most sensational trials ever held in the state, the sordid alliance comprising the political machine, businessmen, and underworld was exposed to public view. All eighteen members of the board of supervisors confessed to accepting bribes. Abe Ruef confessed to receiving bribes from public utilities and businessmen, including $20,000 from Herrin to assist in nominating the Railroad candidate for the United States Senate. He was convicted and sent to prison, but none of the 300 businessmen indicted for giving bribes was convicted. Francis J. Heney, the special prosecutor appointed to handle the case, was shot and seriously wounded in the open court. He was followed by Hiram Johnson, a young attorney who overnight became a leading figure in state politics and was elected governor in 1910 as the candidate of the Progressives. Although the trial aroused public opinion against the boss and machine system and paved the way for the overwhelming victories of the Progressives in state elections, it did little to bring municipal reforms in San Francisco.[8]

In Los Angeles the Southern Pacific–Republican machine, which had long run the city government, suffered a defeat in 1906 by a group of young business and professional men who were interested in good government. Edward A. Dickson, associate editor of the *Los Angeles Express,* published a series of articles and editorials exposing the Southern Pacific's control of the city government. He further attacked the city council for voting to give the Railroad a right of way worth a million dollars without any charge. Dickson led in the formation of a Nonpartisan Committee of One Hundred which, with the support of several municipal reform organizations, nominated a slate of

[8] See Walton Bean, *Boss Ruef's San Francisco* (Berkeley: University of California Press, 1952), Chapters XIII–XV.

candidates in the 1906 municipal election in opposition to the Republican slate. The reform slate was supported by the Republican *Express* and the Democratic *Herald,* but was strongly opposed by the Republican *Times* for disrupting the Republican organization and endangering business interests. The "good government" slate won thirteen seats on the city council but lost the race for mayor. Three years later, in 1909, the reform group won a sweeping victory and secured the adoption of several charter amendments, one of which established nonpartisan city elections.

In 1907 Chester Rowell and Edward A. Dickson formed a statewide organization to work within the Republican party to wrest control from its reactionary leadership and to free it from the domination of the Southern Pacific Railroad. The organization, which at the outset had fewer than 50 members, was called the Lincoln-Roosevelt Republican League. Its first objective was the emancipation of the Republican party, but its larger aim was to purify politics in the state. Opposed to corrupt government and corporation control, it looked to the direct primary, the initiative, the referendum, and the recall as devices by which the voters could overthrow the bosses. Among the other reforms that the League favored were the regulation of utility rates, conservation of forests, outlawing of race-track gambling, workmen's compensation, and minimum wages for women. The similar Populist movement in the Midwest was distinctly agrarian, but the Progressive movement in California was led by independent journalists and lawyers from the metropolitan centers.

Taking advantage of a watered-down direct-primary law passed by the 1909 legislature, the Progressives entered the Republican primary in 1910 with Hiram Johnson as their candidate for governor. He had attracted wide attention because of his prosecution of the sensational Ruef graft cases in San Francisco. The Lincoln-Roosevelt League had carried on a highly efficient publicity campaign for several years, attacking corruption and bossism in the state government. Hiram Johnson stumped the state promising that if elected he would kick the Southern Pacific Railroad out of state government, but saying little else. The

Progressives won an overwhelming victory in the Republican primary, Johnson carrying 53 of the 58 counties, and went on to win the election.

With the vigorous leadership of Governor Johnson and a majority of legislators favorable, legislation was enacted in 1911 and 1913 to carry out the platform pledges of the Progressives. These included a new public-utility law, several conservation measures, strengthening of the direct primary, establishing of the initiative, the referendum, and the recall of public officers, free textbooks for public schools, and several labor-reform bills on which the Progressives were divided. A more vigorous and effective state administration was brought about by the new heads of departments appointed by Governor Johnson, who followed the policy, however, of appointing only his own followers to state office.

In the contest for the Republican nomination for President in 1912, the California delegation actively supported Theodore Roosevelt. Roosevelt was running on a progressive platform against incumbent President William Howard Taft, who had the support of the party conservatives or regulars, as they were called. The national committee, which was controlled by the conservatives, seated the Taft delegations in the numerous election contests, with the result that Taft received the nomination. Charging that the nomination had been stolen, the Roosevelt delegates bolted the convention and formed the new Progressive party, which nominated Roosevelt for President and Hiram Johnson for Vice President.

The new Progressive party was hastily formed in individual states in order that presidential electors pledged to Theodore Roosevelt and Hiram Johnson could be placed on the ballot. It was not necessary to form a Progressive party in California, for the Progressives were firmly in control of the Republican party; their delegates, pledged to Roosevelt and Johnson, ran under the Republican party label. The maneuver was denounced by the Republican press as a fraud on the voters, but not until December, 1913, and after months of debate, did the Progressives cut their ties with the Republican party and form the Progressive party of California. Many Progressive incumbents, having been lifelong Republicans, were unwilling to leave the Republican party and commit their futures to the new Progressive party, whose future was uncertain. Anticipating the formation of the new party, the Progressive-controlled legislature amended the direct-primary law in 1913 by repealing the requirement that a candidate must be a registered member of the party whose nomination he seeks. This change enabled a Progressive to enter the Republican primary as well as the primary of the new Progressive party. Thus was born the unusual provision permitting candidates to cross party lines in the primary election, filing for more than one party's nomination. Cross filing was to have profound effects on California politics for more than forty years.

Few Republican voters changed their registration to the Progressive party, which suffered a severe setback in 1914. Many Progressive-Republicans refused to have anything to do with the new party, but others entered the primaries of both parties as the law permitted. Throughout the country the Progressive party rapidly lost its following and in 1916 received a crushing blow when Theodore Roosevelt declined its nomination for President and urged members to return to the Republican fold. Within a few years it had disappeared.

The influence of the Progressive movement in California continued for at least a decade after it ceased to exist as a political party. It made notable contributions to the politics of the state by curbing the power of the political bosses and machines and the domination of the Republican party by the Southern Pacific Railroad. It instituted higher standards of integrity and decency in government. In 1915 the Progressive legislature enacted a law providing for nonpartisan state elections, but the stalwart Republicans filed a petition requiring a referendum on the measure, and it was defeated in an unusually light vote. Although the voters rejected nonpartisan state elections, cross filing in primary elections muffled partisanship and produced similar results. The great majority of legislators entered the primaries of both parties and won their nominations. The power of the boss and the machine virtually disappeared, for the party organization was no longer able to dictate who would be the nominees of the party. Party caucuses in the state legislature were discontinued and into the political power vacuum moved the lobbyists of special-interest groups, known as the "Third House," who in time came to exercise a control over the legislature comparable to that of the railroads and the political machine of an earlier period.

THE REPUBLICAN ERA

During the booming 1920s California was virtually a one-party state. An occasional Democrat was elected to the state legislature, thanks to the primary law that permitted him to run in the Republican primary as well as that of his own party, but after the defeat of James D. Phelan in 1920 no Democrat was elected to the United States Senate until 1932. The principal election contest was in the Republican primaries, where factions slugged it out. Three governors failed of renomination, but the Democrats were unable to profit by these internal struggles in the Republican party. As late as 1930 the Republicans had more than a two-to-one lead in party registration.

During the New Deal period, when the Democrats were able to carry most of the national elections in the state, they were not able, except briefly, to displace the Republicans in control of the state government. Although the Democrats elected a majority of the California members of Congress from 1932 to 1946, they were never able during this period to control both houses of the California legislature, and only once elected their candidate for governor.

UPTON SINCLAIR'S EPIC MOVEMENT

In 1934 occurred another election which, like that of 1910, proved to be a turning point in California politics. For the first time the Democrats had a majority of the registered voters, with 1,555,705 registered Democrats to 1,430,198 Republicans. If party registration was an indication, the Democrats were now the majority party, and looked forward to the election with confidence.

President Franklin D. Roosevelt was at the height of his popularity, and in 1934 Democrats throughout the country chalked up gains over their landslide victory of 1932. George Creel, a leading Democrat who had served under President Wilson during the First World War, announced his candidacy for the Democratic nomination for governor, confident of being able to defeat colorless Republican Governor Frank F. Merriam. Then occurred a sensational primary and a general election that shook the state from one end to the other and profoundly affected state elections for more than a decade. Upton Sinclair, famous author and frequent Socialist candidate for office, changed his registration to Democratic in the fall of 1933 and shortly afterwards announced his candidacy in a remarkable pamphlet, *I, Governor of California, and How I Ended Poverty.*

Sinclair's plan to "End Poverty in California" (EPIC) proposed the formation of cooperatives to put unemployed people to work on farms and in factories to be provided by the state, and the issuance of scrip money to be used for goods produced in the "production-for-use" cooperatives. EPIC clubs sprang up throughout the state, especially in the southern part, and Sinclair swamped Creel in the Democratic primary by a vote of nearly two to one. Controlling the state Democratic convention, the EPIC delegates wrote a platform that was a slightly diluted version of the EPIC plan. In the election that followed, President Roosevelt and many leading Democrats in the state refused to support the EPIC ticket, which was opposed by a united press throughout the state. It appeared that the Democratic party had been captured by a lunatic fringe. In the election, Governor Merriam was reelected by a large majority and most of the EPIC candidates were defeated, but a number were elected, including Culbert L. Olson, Democratic nominee for state senator from Los Angeles County.

A DEMOCRATIC INTERLUDE

The disastrous defeat of the Democratic party in 1934 after it was taken over by extremists of the left cast a pall over its future.

Although it continued and even increased its majority of registered voters, it was unable to translate these majorities into victories at the polls. In 1936 it won a narrow majority in the state Assembly, which it retained until 1942, but it was not able to win a majority of seats in the Senate. Although in 1938 its candidate for governor, Culbert L. Olson, was elected, the state Senate remained firmly in the hands of the Republicans. Olson soon lost the support of the Democratic Assembly by defections of members of his party and was unable to secure passage of his liberal spending program. After his inept administration had lost public support, he was defeated in 1942 by popular Attorney General Earl Warren, and the Republican party swept back into control of both houses of the legislature. The election of 1942 proved once again that party registration is a poor index of party strength in California elections. Once the practice whereby candidates entered both party primaries became established, the large majority of successful candidates captured the nominations of both parties. There were relatively few contests in the final election. Candidates of both parties conducted essentially nonpartisan campaigns to win state office.

THE WARREN ERA

Under the leadership of Governor Warren the Republicans again returned to a firm control of the state government, electing nearly twice as many members as the Democrats to each house of the state legislature and to Congress during the next decade, and all statewide officers except attorney general. This was a remarkable achievement in view of the fact that during this period the Democrats had a majority of nearly a million registered voters. California presented the extraordinary spectacle of a state with a large Democratic lead in registration that continued until 1956 to elect a large majority of Republicans to the state legislature and to Congress. The low point in the fortunes of the Democratic party was reached in 1946, when Governor Warren captured the Democratic nomination for governor as well as that of his own party, and ran unopposed in the general election. In that year the Democrats lost seven seats in Congress as well as seats in both houses of the state legislature. Four years later, in 1950, James Roosevelt won the Democratic nomination for governor, opposing Earl Warren, who ran for an unprecedented third term and won by a majority of more than a million votes. The Democratic party in the state was thoroughly demoralized, its only successful candidate for state office being Edmund G. (Pat) Brown, who was elected attorney general.

From 1942 until 1953, when his appointment as Chief Justice removed him from California politics, Earl Warren was the most powerful person in state affairs. Although he always conducted his campaigns for state office as a nonpartisan, Earl Warren nevertheless dominated the Republican party for nearly twenty years. For a brief period he was state chairman, but party activities and party loyalty held little attraction for him.

Twice in his career Warren captured the nomination of the Democratic party as well as that of the Republicans—in 1938 as candidate for attorney general and in 1946 as candidate for reelection as governor. Although supported by the three largest conservative Republican newspapers in the state, Warren espoused liberal reform measures such as old-age pensions, workmen's compensation, health insurance, prison reform, mental hospitals, and welfare legislation. He assumed the liberal, progressive mantle formerly worn by Hiram Johnson. He gave the state a competent, forward-looking administration with high *esprit de corps*. As a candidate for attorney general and three times for governor, he appealed not only to the conservative voters but also to the liberal prolabor voters in the metropolitan centers of the state. For his liberalism he earned the opposition of the conservative wing of the Republican party, which fought his progressive measures in the legislature and finally contested the delegation which placed his name in nomination for President at the Republican national convention in 1952.

Warren was keenly aware of the dominant forces in California politics: the large proportion of independent voters; the necessity of a candidate for governor to appeal to the liberal urban vote as well as to the conservative elements in the state. He followed essentially a middle-of-the-road course which was equally displeasing to the extreme right and the extreme left, but was agreeable to the large body of voters in between. He was able to retain the support of both organized labor and the business community.

Warren's retirement from California politics in 1953 to become Chief Justice of the United States left the Republican party without any generally accepted leader. For several years there ensued a struggle for leadership among United States Senator William F. Knowland, Governor Goodwin J. Knight, and Vice President Richard M. Nixon. In the Democratic landslide in 1958 both Knowland and Knight were decisively defeated at the polls, leaving Nixon the undisputed leader of his party in the state. Nixon suffered a similar defeat when he ran for governor in 1962 against Democratic incumbent Edmund G. Brown; he then announced his retirement from politics and moved outside the state. In recent years the Republicans have been beset with internal struggles for leadership between the moderates and right-wing groups, without a recognized state leader able to reconcile the factional differences and achieve the unity that is essential for victories at the polls.

DEMOCRATIC VICTORIES

In 1958 the Democrats swept into state offices with a landslide victory, winning all state offices except secretary of state, and large majorities in both houses of the state legislature. This was the first real Democratic victory in state elections for more than sixty years, although the party had enjoyed a large majority of registered voters after 1936. Facing a badly divided Republican party, Brown defeated Knowland in the race for governor by more than a million votes. The Democrats maintained their majorities in the state legislature and Congress in 1960. In 1962, aided by the Democratic reapportionment of the preceding year, they gained nine new members of Congress, including seven of the members elected to the eight new seats allocated to California, and five members of the state Assembly.

In 1958 incumbent Republican Governor Goodwin J.

Knight planned to run for reelection, but because of pressure upon him by large party contributors to give way to Senator William F. Knowland, he reluctantly withdrew from the race for governor and filed for the United States Senate. Though Knowland and Knight won their party's nominations without difficulty, both lost by large majorities to Democratic opponents in the general election. The switch of offices led to strained relations between the two leading candidates and a divided party when unity was essential to victory. Another factor in the Republican defeat was the bitter contest over the "right to work" initiative proposition on the ballot. Knowland and some other Republican candidates supported the measure while Knight and others refused to align themselves with the opponents of the union shop. Organized labor turned out its vote in force and swelled the Democratic majorities.

In 1959 Governor Brown was successful in pushing through the Democratic legislature his legislative program of "responsible liberalism." Many of the newly elected Democratic legislators had campaigned on a promise to support Brown's legislative program. Brown's leadership of his party, however, declined in 1960 when he was unable to swing the Democratic delegation at the national convention to Kennedy for President on the eve of the convention. Despite the increasing partisanship of the state legislature in recent years, Brown has faced increasing difficulties in securing the enactment of his legislative program. Assemblyman Jesse M. Unruh, a rising power in the Democratic party from Los Angeles and the dominant leader of the state Assembly, has often differed with Brown over his legislative recommendations. The independence of the legislature from control by the governor, however, is not new in California. The strongest governors, including Earl Warren, were often unable to secure the passage of their recommendations by the legislature, especially bills opposed by powerful special-interest groups.

THE 1962 STATE ELECTION

In 1962 the Republican party made a strong bid to recapture control of the state government, nominating Richard M. Nixon for governor.[4] Nixon, its leading vote getter, had never been defeated in the state. As presidential candidate he carried California in 1960 (though by a narrow majority—35,623; 50.3 percent), a generally Democratic year. The party was severely handicapped, however, by three facts: (1) the Democrats had a lead in party registration of more than a million voters; (2) the state in 1961 had been redistricted by the Democratic legislature, greatly to the advantage of the Democrats; and (3) nearly two-thirds of the members of both houses of the legislature and four of the five elective partisan statewide officers were Democrats. In addition, a growing struggle between the moderates and conservatives in the Republican party threatened to disrupt its unity.

The Republican primary in 1962 was marked by numerous contests between moderates and conservatives, although in previous elections the party had usually been able to agree upon a single candidate for each office before the primary election. When the favored candidate received the nod from the party leadership and was endorsed by the influential California Republican Assembly (CRA), other Republican aspirants had almost always withdrawn from the race. It was the tradition of the party to nominate moderate candidates for statewide offices, candidates who would appeal to labor and urban voters, in order to overcome the large Democratic lead in registration. Conservatives were often nominated for the state legislature and for Congress. A compromise was thus reached whereby the moderates received most of the nominations for leading statewide offices while conservatives dominated in the selection of Republican legislative candidates and in the determination of party policies.

The CRA state convention in 1962, which met to endorse candidates for statewide offices, was marked by hot contests between moderates and conservatives. Breaking with tradition, the conservative candidates, who polled about one-third of the convention vote, refused to withdraw from the race. They entered the primary, not expecting to win but rather to continue the

---

[4] For an excellent, detailed analysis, see Totton J. Anderson and Eugene C. Lee, "The 1962 Election in California," 16 *Western Political Quarterly* 396–420 (1963).

fight for control of the party. The leading race in the Republican primary was between Richard Nixon, who a year earlier had announced that he would not enter the race for governor, and Joseph C. Shell, a successful Los Angeles oil man and militant conservative, formerly Republican floor leader of the state Assembly. Nixon entered the race for governor with the support of many prominent Republicans who thought that only he could defeat Democrat Edmund G. Brown. Thus he gambled his political fortune on the results of this election. As governor he would strengthen his position as titular leader of his national party and would be in a commanding position to win the nomination for President in 1964, but a defeat would imperil his political future.

Nixon no doubt hoped to receive the unified support of all factions of the party, but he faced instead strong opposition to his nomination by Shell and also by former Governor Goodwin J. Knight, who was forced to withdraw from the race because of illness. Shell conducted a vigorous and well-financed campaign throughout the state in which he maintained that Nixon could not defeat Brown. Confident of winning, and desiring not to offend the conservatives who supported Shell, Nixon disregarded Shell's attack and concentrated his attack on Brown and his administration. Shell polled one-third of the primary vote, thus demonstrating the strength of the conservatives. Yet Senator Thomas Kuchel, who was opposed by two prominent conservatives, polled more than 75 percent of the primary vote, running strongest in the northern part of the state.

Only one of the four Democratic incumbents in statewide offices was opposed in the primary, but there were many contests for nomination for members of the state legislature and Representatives in Congress, except in districts where Democratic incumbents were running for reelection. A considerable number of voters, accustomed to voting for candidates of the opposite party in primary elections, wrote in their names.

The 1962 campaign for governor was one of the most hotly contested in the history of the state and one of the dirtiest campaigns that California voters have ever witnessed. The candidates discussed some of the major issues facing the state and outlined broad programs to deal with the pressing problems of conservation, urban sprawl, agriculture, education, welfare, and other concerns; but the campaign soon degenerated into an exchange of personal attacks as both sides charged the opposition with smear tactics and the circulation of false reports and innuendos. Several anonymous political publications were restrained by court order from being circulated.

Nixon's strategy was dictated by the facts that the Democrats enjoyed a lead of more than a million registered voters, and that to overcome this lead he needed to win the votes of 20 to 25 percent of the Democrats who voted and to retain at least 90 percent of the Republican votes. A heavy Republican turnout and a light Democratic vote, which often occurs in state elections, would help to offset the Democratic lead in registration. The dramatic campaign, however, which monopolized the campaign news, resulted in an unusually heavy vote.

In order to win the unified support of the Republican party, Nixon took steps to shore up the party organization throughout the state, to heal wounds created in the primary contests, and to secure the support of all factions and leaders of the party, while avoiding any statements that would alienate independent voters and conservative Democrats. To avoid endorsing several Republican candidates for Congress who were avowed members of the John Birch Society (which would have offended many voters of both parties), Nixon announced that as a candidate for a state office he would not endorse any candidate for Congress—a stand which did not endear him to Republican candidates for Congress.

The tactic successfully used by Earl Warren and Goodwin Knight in their campaigns for governor had been to conduct a nonpartisan campaign, enlisting the support of organized labor and prominent Democrats and appealing to urban voters of both parties. Because of his recognized leadership of the Republican party in the nation as well as in California, Nixon was unable to present a convincing nonpartisan image but did select issues and campaign appeals that would appeal to conservative voters of both parties. He devoted his campaign largely to a personal attack on Brown and his administration, accusing Brown of nepotism and representing him as a bumbling, indecisive, and incompetent administrator surrounded by political appointees. Nixon made numerous charges of mismanagement and maladministration under Brown, and asserted that he was responsible for the high rate of crime in the state because of his failure to support law-enforcement agencies. This latter accusation backfired when local law-enforcement officials praised Brown's record and disputed Nixon's statistics purporting to show that California had the highest crime rate in the country.

Brown's strategy was to present the image of a forceful, decisive, competent, and experienced executive, engaged in important business as the governor of the largest state. He attacked Nixon as being a man unacquainted with the problems of the state because of his long absence, whose primary interest was to run for President again, and referred to him as the "Prospector from the Potomac," who wanted to make a quick stake in order to return to Washington, D.C.

The early public-opinion polls indicated that Nixon had a substantial lead over Brown. Near the end of the campaign, however, they indicated that Brown was ahead. Nixon and his campaign organization then raised the familiar charge of communism against the Brown administration. Nixon disavowed any accusation that Brown was a communist, but asserted that some of his assistants were "soft" on communism and that Brown was the "captive" of the liberally oriented California Democratic Council, which Nixon represented as a dangerous left-wing organization. The communism charges, which Nixon had successfully used in campaigns prior to 1960, were doubtless introduced into the campaign as appeals to all Republicans and conservative Democrats, but it is doubtful that they gained votes in 1962. California voters were not easily persuaded that Brown, a well-known Catholic, was soft on communism or that there existed any real danger of communism in the state service.

When the votes were counted the Democrats had won again. Brown was reelected by 300,000 votes and the three other Democratic incumbents in state offices were also reelected. Thanks to the Democratic redistricting of the state in 1961, the Democrats gained five seats in the state Assembly and nine seats in Congress, including seven of the eight new seats. Although the Republicans gained in the popular vote over 1960, they lost seats in the state Assembly and in Congress, gaining only in the state Senate. The major victory of the Republicans was the reelection of United States Senator Thomas Kuchel by a majority of 700,000 in this Democratic year, illustrating again the independence of the California voter.

The 1962 election indicated again the high cost of political campaigning in the state. Brown and Nixon each spent approximately a half million dollars in the primary campaign, and Shell spent slightly more. The organizations conducting the campaign for Brown and Nixon before the election each spent about $1½ million, the largest expenditure being for radio and television, amounting to nearly $1 million. Both parties were able to mount well-financed campaigns, conducted by professionals. The employment of 11,000 paid political workers by the Democrats in Los Angeles County aroused a storm of controversy.

THE 1964 PRIMARY AND GENERAL ELECTION [5]

In the California presidential primary election in June, 1964, the last primary held before the Republican national convention, the Republican delegates were won by Senator Goldwater of Arizona in a bitter struggle between the party's moderates and its right-wing conservatives. Goldwater's victory in the California primary, which gave him its large bloc of 86 delegates, assured him the Republican nomination for President despite last-minute efforts by Republican moderates to block his nomination. There was no contest for the Democratic presidential nomination, but

---

[5] The following account draws heavily on the excellent analysis of the election by Totton J. Anderson and Eugene C. Lee, "The 1964 Election in California," 18 *Western Political Quarterly* 451–474 (1965).

two slates of delegates were entered in the primary, one headed by Governor Brown, which won by more than two to one, and a second delegation headed by Mayor Yorty of Los Angeles.

Several weeks before the California primary Governor Nelson Rockefeller of New York had won a surprising victory in Oregon, where Goldwater ran a poor third. A month before the national convention Goldwater had gone far ahead in the number of pledged delegates and needed only the California delegation to give him the required majority. Rockefeller's victory in Oregon encouraged moderate Republicans that there was still a chance to stop the Goldwater bandwagon. A Rockefeller victory in California would have dealt a crushing blow to Goldwater's chance of nomination, but would not necessarily have assured the nomination of Rockefeller; the effect could have been to deadlock the convention and lead to the nomination of another candidate acceptable to all factions of the party. It was probably for this reason that the Republican press in California gave its support to Rockefeller in the primary campaign. Both parties, as a rule, follow the practice of choosing their presidential candidates from the center rather than from the extreme right or left wing, but in 1964 the Republicans broke with tradition and nominated a candidate who was identified with the conservative wing of the party.

Goldwater had entered the California primary early, appointing an advisory committee headed by former United States Senator William F. Knowland, editor of the *Oakland Tribune*. After his candidacy was formally announced, his campaign was conducted by Citizens for Goldwater-Miller committee, headed by movie and television actor Ronald Reagan and the head of a large citrus-marketing organization. (The name of the committee indicated that Goldwater had already chosen his running mate.) The Goldwater campaign, organized throughout the state, opened offices in each of the 58 counties and 50 offices in Los Angeles County alone.

Both Rockefeller and Goldwater conducted well-financed campaigns with reported expenditure of $3½ million each—undoubtedly the largest campaign expenditure on record in the state. On the day before the election, newspapers in the San Joaquin valley carried as many as five large advertisements for Goldwater in a single issue.

The Rockefeller campaign was headed by United States Senator Thomas Kuchel, former Governor Goodwin J. Knight, George Christopher, former mayor of San Francisco, and other prominent moderates. The Rockefeller forces attacked Goldwater for his stands on the United Nations, social security, civil rights, and the use of nuclear weapons, and for the association of his campaign with the John Birch Society. The Goldwater campaign, however, centered its attack on the Johnson administration, seeking to avoid the internal conflict between the moderates and conservatives. The contest became more bitter as the day of the primary approached. Headquarters of each candidate received anonymous telephone threats of bombs; in one county the Rockefeller headquarters was forced to hire private detectives in order to stay open. Eleven of the fifteen Republican congressmen from the state signed a statement that the contest had crossed the "narrow line between healthy controversy and destructive charges."

A poll conducted a few days before the primary indicated that Rockefeller was leading by 9 percent of the Republican voters, a lead ordinarily sufficient to assure victory, but the poll indicated also that the Goldwater voters felt much more strongly about the race than the Rockefeller voters. Goldwater's victory was probably due to the heavier turnout of voters favoring him. A surprising indication of the poll was that 50 percent of the Republican voters did not favor either candidate, a portent of the Republican defeat in the ensuing election.

Goldwater won the primary election with a majority of 68,000 votes in a total vote of more than 2,000,000. His victory was due to the large majorities that he received in Los Angeles County and adjoining Orange County, which together have 45 percent of the Republican voters in the state. Goldwater polled 60 percent of the Republican vote in Los Angeles County, piling up a 167,000 majority. In Orange County he received twice as many votes as Rockefeller, a 50,000 majority. He carried only 14 of the state's 58 counties, but these included all of the populous southern counties except Santa Barbara. Rockefeller carried the northern counties with a majority of 172,000 votes, but these were not sufficient to overcome the 240,000 lead of Goldwater in the southern counties. The primary followed the same pattern of voting which has marked recent California elections, with the right-wing conservative Republicans strongest in the south and the moderate Republicans strongest in the north.

The Goldwater victory was a significant turn in the fight between the moderates and conservatives to control the Republican party, which had marked the 1962 primary and election, and continued into 1966. In 1963 the conservatives captured control of the Young Republicans convention, which a year later endorsed Goldwater for President by a vote of 256½ to 33½ and refused to pledge support if any other candidate received the nomination. A group of militant conservatives formed the United Republicans of California (UROC) to promote conservative policies and candidates. In 1964 UROC, which claimed a membership of 10,000, refused to endorse 14 of the 28 Republican members of the state Assembly because their voting records were not considered sufficiently conservative. In 1964 the conservative wing of the party won control of the influential California Republican Assembly, which for thirty years had virtually controlled the Republican nominations by its preprimary endorsement of candidates.

The conservatives failed, however, in their attempt in 1964 to capture control of the Republican State Central Committee, the official organization of the party. Caspar Weinberger, chairman of the Republican State Central Committee and a moderate, declared that the attempt was "an effort . . . by a small, narrowly based, and heavily financed group to take over the official committees of the California Republican party." [6] The Demo-

---

[6] Anderson and Lee, "The 1964 Election," p. 458.

cratic-controlled legislature came to the aid of the Republican moderates and revised the state law to give each party incumbent in office, including legislators, the power to appoint nine members of the state central committee instead of five previously provided by law.

The ultraconservative Republicans were even less successful in electing their members to public office. Anderson and Lee reported that six Republican candidates, two for Congress, one for the state Senate, and one for the Assembly, were identified by the press as members of the John Birch Society. All but one were defeated.[7]

Lyndon Johnson carried the state for President with a majority of nearly 1,300,000 votes, receiving 59.2 percent of the total vote. In northern California he polled 65 percent of the vote, in Los Angeles County 58 percent, and 51 percent in other southern counties. According to the widely respected *California Poll,* fewer than 10 percent of Democratic voters switched to Goldwater, but Johnson received one-fourth of the votes cast by Republicans. The Republicans who switched to Johnson were most numerous in the middle- and lower-income groups, persons under 60 years of age, and those who resided in the northern part of the state.

In other states the landslide victory of Lyndon Johnson carried with it the defeat of many popular Republican candidates for Congress and state legislatures. This effect does not appear to have been experienced in California, although a more popular presidential candidate would undoubtedly have increased the vote received by other Republican candidates. As is indicated below, in the large number of safe legislative districts in California the reelection of incumbents of each party is virtually assured, irrespective of the presidential race. Only in close districts is the popularity of the head of the ticket able to affect the outcome of legislative contests. The 1964 election indicated the high degree of independence of California voters and their widespread practice of voting split tickets.

---

[7] Anderson and Lee, "The 1964 Election," p. 451.

Polling approximately 47 percent of the vote cast for legislative offices, Republican candidates won 15 of the 38 seats in Congress and 31 of the 80 seats in the state Assembly. The Republicans gained three seats in the Assembly, but the number of seats held by each party in Congress and the state Senate was not changed. The Democrats, who polled approximately 53 percent of the vote, won substantial majorities in each house of the state legislature and in Congress in consequence of the advantage which they gained through the partisan reapportionment of 1961.

The striking features of the legislative elections in 1964 were: (1) the large number of incumbents who were reelected; and (2) the large number of safe districts. Of the 38 members of Congress, 36 sought reelection and all but two were elected. Of the 20 state senators, 19 whose terms expired in 1964 ran for reelection and all were elected. Of the 80 members of the Assembly, 76 were candidates and 70 were reelected. Legislative incumbents, who are usually well known throughout their districts, have a great advantage over opponents who are not so widely known. In addition, many legislators, especially members of Congress, have rendered to constituents many services which gain their active support.

A district is considered ordinarily to be safe if the winning candidate polls 55 percent of the vote cast. (It may be noted that President Johnson, who carried California by a landslide majority, polled only 59.2 percent of the vote.) In 1964 only five members elected to Congress from California received less than 55 percent of the vote; the other 33 members received 55 percent of the vote or more. The winning candidate in 17 of the 20 state senatorial districts holding elections and in 69 of the 80 state Assembly districts were elected by 55 percent or more of the vote cast for the office. Eighty-five percent of the legislative districts were safe. Most legislators were elected by overwhelming majorities. Twenty-five members elected to Congress received 50 percent more votes than their opponents; 16 received twice as many. The statistics for the state legislature are similar.

The practice of creating safe legislative districts is a serious threat to the two-party system and deprives voters in most districts of an effective choice in the election of their legislative representatives. It is a product of partisan redistricting of the state by the party in control of the state legislature.

THE 1966 PRIMARY AND GENERAL ELECTION

After the 1964 election Republicans were generally agreed that it was necessary to end intraparty fights and present a united front in the 1966 election in order to win the office of governor, the leading political prize, and possibly other state executive offices. Short of a landslide victory, they had little hope of electing a majority of the members of either house of the state legislature or the House of Representatives, for the Democrats held about two-thirds of the seats and enjoyed the great advantage of having reapportioned the state in 1961 and 1965. The large majority of the legislative districts were safely Democratic. Consequently, attention in the 1966 primary and election centered largely on the office of governor.

The need for party unity was strongly urged at Republican meetings in 1965. State chairman Dr. Gaylord B. Parkinson issued a stern warning to Republican candidates not to speak ill of each other, saying that "if any Republican candidate is so misguided as to attack another Republican candidate he will suffer severe reverses, his financial resources will dry up, and he will be rejected at the polls." [8]

Senator Thomas H. Kuchel, who had been reelected in 1962 by more than 700,000 majority, was urged to enter the race against Governor Edmund G. Brown, but withdrew his name in September, 1965, and issued a statement attacking extremists in the party. The first candidate to enter the race for the Republican nomination for governor was television and movie star Ronald Reagan, cochairman of the Goldwater-Miller campaign organization in California in 1964. Before announcing his candi-

---

[8] *Christian Science Monitor*, Sept. 28, 1965, p. 10.

dacy, Reagan toured the state in 1965, addressing enthusiastic Republican audiences. He was the overwhelming choice of the California Republican Assembly, United Republicans of California, and other conservative groups, and early in the race attained a substantial lead in the public polls, which he maintained throughout the campaign.

Saying that he would not speak a single word against any other Republican candidate, Reagan limited his primary-campaign speeches to an attack on the Brown administration. He viewed with alarm the growing crime rate and crime in the streets, the mounting cost of state government which he promised to reduce by at least $245,000,000 annually, the burden of California's public-welfare program, high taxes, swollen bureaucracy, and "planners" in state government. He attacked federal centralization and the "Great Society" program, which he linked with Brown, and proposed instead a "Creative Society" in which "the people themselves would have the strength and ability to solve the problems that confront us." He opposed legislation prohibiting racial discrimination in housing, and came out in favor of a return to the *bracero* program of farm labor.

Reagan quickly proved to be an attractive, articulate, and effective campaigner. The early image of him as an actor was replaced by an image of him as a leading candidate for governor, conservative but not extremist in his views. In his speeches he stressed issues which had the greatest audience appeal, such as the "shameful things going on" at the University of California at Berkeley; he promised to investigate these and to fire those responsible. In reply to the charge that he did not have experience which would qualify him to become governor, he said that he was not a politician, contending that common sense rather than politics was needed to solve the pressing problems of the state.

The candidate favored by the leading moderate Republicans for the Republican gubernatorial nomination was George Christopher, former mayor of San Francisco and Republican candidate for lieutenant governor in 1962. In the polls of Republicans during the campaign he trailed Reagan, but led him in the polls of Democrats and independent voters. Christopher was the Republican candidate whom the polls indicated had the best chance to defeat Brown in the general election.

Christopher, obeying the Parkinson injunction not to speak ill of a Republican opponent, conducted one of the most ineffective campaigns in California political history. Only by a vigorous attack on Reagan could he have overcome the early lead that Reagan's well-organized campaign had secured, but such an attack might have backfired because of the opposition to intraparty fights. A report of the conviction of the Christopher dairy firm in 1943 of violating a milk-price regulation, which Drew Pearson published in the last week of the campaign, evidently lost many votes for Christopher.

Governor Brown did not announce his candidacy until early 1966, but it was widely assumed in 1965 that he would seek a third term. Only Earl Warren had ever been elected for a third term as governor, and in the history of the state only three other governors had been reelected to a second term. Brown's old opponent, Mayor Samuel Yorty of Los Angeles, who had recently been reelected by a large majority, entered the Democratic primary against Brown. In 1964 Yorty had led a slate of candidates for delegates to the Democratic national convention in opposition to the slate led by Brown, and polled about one-third of the vote. In 1962 he bolted the Democratic ticket to support Nixon for governor against Brown, and in 1960 he supported Nixon for President.

Although Yorty did not expect to win, his candidacy for the Democratic nomination for governor provided him with a forum for attacking Brown. He conducted a well-financed, hard-hitting campaign against Brown and his administration, charging him with failure to solve the perennial problems of government— crime, law enforcement, public welfare, race relations, smog, transportation, high cost of government, taxation, and others. In the closing days of the campaign he accused Brown and his aides of being soft on Communism. Yorty continued his attacks until election day, appealing to all dissident groups within the party, especially those who were unhappy about housing legislation, the civil-rights movement, and the Watts riots.

Brown made no reply to Yorty's charges, nor did he counter by pointing to some of the unsolved problems in Yorty's own backyard. Instead, he devoted his campaign to a defense of his administration during his two terms as governor and emphasized the progress made in the state. In response to Reagan's attack on his administration, Brown charged Reagan with "sailing a pure Goldwater" course of right-wing conservatism. He stated further that in the general-election campaign he would make an issue of Reagan's lack of the experience that would qualify him to be governor.

The primary results proved to be surprising in both parties. Brown, who was expected to poll about twice the vote received by Yorty, received only 53 percent of the Democratic vote cast, while Yorty polled 34.5 percent; 12.5 was polled by four other protest candidates. Reagan, who was expected to win the Republican primary by a large majority, polled more than twice as many votes as his leading opponent, Christopher. Reagan piled up large majorities in the south and carried all but five of the northern counties. The outcome was widely interpreted as a protest vote against the policies of the Brown administration, and a definite trend toward conservatism in both parties.

Two weeks after the primary election a poll showed that Reagan was leading by 52 percent of the voters polled to 37 percent for Brown and 11 percent undecided. In 1962, when the issues were much the same as in 1966, Brown overcame an early lead by Nixon in the public polls, but the disaffection in the Democratic ranks appeared much greater in 1966 than in 1962.

A record number of 788 candidates entered the two party primaries for the six partisan state executive offices and 158 seats in the state legislature and the House of Representatives. Nominations for all state offices except treasurer were contested in both parties, although in all cases incumbents won over their opponents by large majorities. In legislative districts where there was no incumbent candidate, ten or more candidates for the party nomination was not uncommon. No longer were candidates who failed to receive the unofficial party endorsement deterred from entering the primary.

All 37 present members of the House of Representatives (one seat was vacant) were renominated. Of the 16 "peace" candidates, mostly Democrats, five were nominated, including three incumbents, and several others polled about 40 percent of the vote. With few exceptions, state legislators who entered the primary were nominated; 20 assemblymen ran for the nomination for the state Senate and 17 were successful.

The election campaign continued the debate over the same issues that were raised in the primary campaign. Governor Brown defended the progressive record of his administration, stressing the huge water plan in which he had taken the leadership, the adoption of a comprehensive plan for higher education in the state, and the fact that state taxes had not been raised for seven years. He claimed credit for the booming California economy and the righer rate of employment than when he took office.

Brown stepped up his charges that Reagan was the candidate of the right wing of the Republican party and attacked him for failing to disavow the support of the John Birch Society. The attempt to portray Reagan as a right-wing extremist, however, proved to be unsuccessful and was largely abandoned during the closing weeks of the campaign. Reagan and his campaign managers had succeeded in projecting an image of him as a friendly, articulate man of conservative but not extremist views on public issues.

As the campaign was nearing its end, Brown shifted his attack to Reagan's lack of public experience, asserting that "no man in the history of the state had ever tried to run for governor with less experience." The great majority of voters were unimpressed, although *Life* magazine and the Republican *San Francisco Chronicle* announced support of Brown for this reason. Reagan met the attack head on, professing proudly that he was not a "professional politician" (implying that Brown was) and maintaining that what was needed in state government was the application of common sense and good judgment of laymen rather than the professional qualities of politicians.

At the outset of the campaign Reagan took steps to unite the party, inviting leading moderates who had supported George Christopher in the primary campaign to join his campaign organization. As in the primary campaign, Reagan proved to be a formidable campaigner, continuing his attacks on the Brown administration for high taxes, lowered morality, and bureaucracy. A trained public speaker, slim, handsome, always smiling, he addressed enthusiastic audiences wherever he went, and toward the end of the campaign devoted much of his effort to aiding his running mates. In a speech which rubbed all of the social raw spots that seemed to bother the voters, he criticized public welfare for perpetuating poverty instead of curing its causes and promised to enlist the cooperation of business in providing jobs for the unemployed. He attacked the Brown administration for being "soft" on crime, for "usurpation" of local authority, for permitting federal meddling in state and local affairs, and for a decline in public morality.

Reagan stated that the main difference between his viewpoint and that of Brown was that "the Governor turns to government for answers to problems. I turn to the private sector." Advocating a "Creative Society," he promised that if elected he would find ways to turn problems back to the people and local governments to solve with the aid of the state and to cut the "bureacratic fat" out of the state budget. He attacked the high cost of state government but advocated state assumption of a larger part of the cost of education in order to relieve local property taxpayers.

Reagan tempered his attack on the University of California, Berkeley campus, by giving assurances that he would keep politics out of the administration of the university, and accused Brown of injecting politics into university affairs. Both candidates disavowed making any appeal to the white backlash, but in the closing weeks of the campaign Brown accused Reagan of "riding the backlash wave" by subtle appeals to this vote in his attacks on welfare administration, crime, and riots, and in his unqualified opposition to the Rumford antidiscrimination housing act. Brown attempted to placate opponents of the Rumford act by promising to appoint a citizen commission to inquire into the problem and to recommend revisions of the act.

The public-opinion polls at the end of the campaign indicated that Reagan had maintained his lead of about 6 percent, which he had held since September, but that 10 percent of the voters were undecided. In the final vote Reagan won by a majority of more than 900,000, leading Brown by 57.5 percent to 42.5 percent. Robert H. Finch, Republican candidate for Lieutenant Governor, led the ticket, polling nearly 60 percent of the vote against Glenn M. Anderson, Democratic incumbent. The Republican landslide victory carried the other Republican candidates into state office by small majorities; only the office of Attorney General was retained by the Democratic incumbent, Thomas C. Lynch. The results of the election were similar to 1954, when the Democrats had won only the office of Attorney General.

The Republican party gained 7 seats in the State Assembly and 6 seats in the new Senate. The Democrats, greatly aided by the Democratic reapportionment of the state, retained a narrow majority of 42–38 in the Assembly and 21–19 in the Senate. Speaker Jesse M. Unruh, who was regarded as a shoo in, squeaked through with a slim majority over his Republican opponent.

Different explanations were offered of the Republican landslide victory, though all agreed that two-party politics had returned to California. It should be noted, however, that the Republican party polled almost as many votes as the Democrats for legislative offices in 1962 and 1964. Reagan attributed the Republican victory to the desire of the people for a "pause" and to the fact that the Republican party was united. Attorney General Lynch, maintaining that the defeat of Brown was due primarily to the backlash vote, deplored votes cast on the basis of racial prejudice. Election analysts pointed to the striking similarities in the 1966 election results with the vote on Proposition 14 in 1964. Four State Supreme Court Justices who had voted to hold Proposition 14 unconstitutional received more than 1.3 million "No" votes after an organized campaign to defeat them—an indication of the strong disapproval by many voters of legislation prohibiting racial discrimination in housing.

PARTY TRENDS IN REGISTRATION AND ELECTIONS

After the disappearance of the short-lived Progressive party, California returned to the Republican fold and during the 1920s became virtually a one-party state. Two-thirds of the voters were registered as Republicans and only one-fourth as Democrats, the remainder declining to state any party affiliation. The Republican party was so dominant in the state that the Democrats had difficulty in finding candidates to run for public office. Republican candidates increasingly entered both primaries and often won both nominations. The few Democrats in the state legislature were elected, as a rule, because they had captured the Republican nomination.

The Great Depression of the 1930s brought about a party revolution in California as in many other states. Thousands of Republicans switched their party affiliation and new voters flocked to the Democratic party. By 1934 a majority of California voters were registered as Democrats; by 1936 the ratio had increased to 58 percent. The party has since retained this substantial lead, except for a small decline in the 1950s. The Democrats, however, were not able until 1958 to translate this large majority of registered voters into solid election victories. Though they carried the state for President in the five presidential elections from 1932 through 1948, they failed during this period to win control of the state government. Democrats held the majority of the state's seats in the House of Representatives from 1932 to 1946, when the Republicans went into the lead, which they held until 1958.

In the decade following the Second World War the Democratic party suffered repeated major defeats at the hands of the Republican party headed by popular, liberal Governor Earl

Warren. In 1952 the Republicans elected two-thirds of the members of the state Assembly, three-fourths of the members of the state Senate, and 19 of the 30 members of the House of Representatives. The fortunes of politics, however, often change rapidly. Six years later in 1958 the Democratic party swept into control in the state, electing Edmund G. Brown governor, winning all other elective state offices except secretary of state, and electing large majorities in both houses of the legislature. The party maintained its legislative majority in 1960 and was thus able to redistrict the state to its advantage, making it difficult if not impossible for the Republicans to capture control of the legislature and the congressional delegation in the 1960s.

TABLE I. REGISTRATION OF VOTERS IN CALIFORNIA,
1932–1966

		Percent		
Year	Total (Thousands)	Democratic	Republican	Others (Including "Declined to State")
1932	2,889	40	54	6
1936	3,253	58	38	4
1940	4,052	60	36	4
1944	4,141	58.5	37.5	4
1948	5,061	57	38	5
1952	5,998	55	41	4
1954	5,885	56	41	3
1956	6,409	56	41	3
1958	6,752	57.4	39.6	3
1960	7,465	57.5	39.2	3.3
1962	7,531	57.0	39.9	3.1
1964	8,184	57.9	38.9	3.2
1966	8,340	56.6	40.2	2.7

In the 1964 general election the Democratic party had a total of 4,737,886 registered voters (57.9 percent) to 3,181,272 registered Republicans (38.9 percent). The Republicans led in only four counties: the populous suburban counties of Orange in the south and Marin in the north, and two mountain counties—Alpine and Mono—with a combined registration of fewer than two thousand voters. Seven other counties in which the Democrats had a lead of 50 to 55 percent, however, may be classified as Republican: Lake, Mariposa, Riverside, San Diego, Santa Barbara, Santa Cruz, and Sutter. The remaining 47 counties in which the Democrats have 55 percent or more of the registered voters may be classified as close, leaning Democratic, or safe Democratic, depending on the extent of the lead of the Democrats in the registration. Several Republican congressmen were reelected in 1964 by large majorities from districts which had 60 percent or more Democratic registration.

TABLE II. CALIFORNIA'S VOTE FOR PRESIDENT, 1932–1964

Year	Democratic		Republican		Minor Parties	
	Vote (Thousands)	Per-cent	Vote (Thousands)	Per-cent	Vote (Thousands)	Per-cent
1932	1,324	57	848	37	116	5
1936	1,766	67	836	32	35	1
1940	1,878	57	1,351	41	40	1
1944	1,988	57	1,513	43	19	*
1948	1,913	48	1,895	47	213	5
1952	2,198	42	2,897	57	44	*
1956	2,420	44	3,028	55	17	*
1960	3,224	49.6	3,259	50.1	29	*
1964	4,171	59.2	2,879	40.8	5	*

* Less than 1 percent of the total vote.

PARTY VICTORIES: RETROSPECT AND PROSPECT

Despite the large Democratic lead in the number of registered voters after 1934, the Republican party continued to win state elections for more than twenty years except for a brief period at the end of the 1930s, electing practically all state officers, a large majority of the members of the state legislature, and after 1942 a majority of the state's members of the House of Representatives. Valuable insights into California politics and the voting behavior of its citizens may be gained by an understanding of why the Republican party was able with a minority of the registered voters to retain its control of the state government, and how the Democrats were finally able in 1958 to win a solid victory.

Party registration in California is an unreliable measure of party strength, as the election results over thirty years abundantly indicate. Many voters regard themselves as independents, especially in state and local elections, although to vote in primary elections they are required to register as party members. Those who decline to state a party affiliation disqualify themselves to vote in these most important elections. Most contests are decided in the primary election rather than in the general election. Many California voters are newcomers to the state and have formed no definite political allegiance in the community in which they have settled; they register as partisans but vote as independents. Many register as Democrats because they come from areas that are strongly Democratic, but that past does not mean that they continue their lightly felt party affiliation, though they may not bother to change their party registration.

The Democratic registration is highest in the low-income, less-educated, and minority groups, many of whom are politically apathetic and often fail to vote. The higher turnout of Republican voters tends to offset their fewer numbers. In addition, public polls indicate that a large number of Democrats, as a rule, cross party lines in elections and vote for candidates of the opposing party. Because of the Democratic lead in registration, it is recognized that Republican candidates in most areas and those who are running for statewide offices must win a considerable number of Democrats and independents in order to be elected. Republican candidates are nominated who will appeal to many Democratic voters and independents. Often they are better known than their Democratic opponents, have stronger financial support, and are able to conduct more effective and better-publicized campaigns. In addition, they enjoy the support and publicity provided by the Republican press, an important asset.

The primary law which until 1960 permitted candidates to enter the primaries of both parties was an important factor in

Republican victories. Cross filing tended to weaken political parties and to introduce a form of nonpartisanship in state elections. Almost all candidates entered both party primaries and many uninformed voters unwittingly voted for candidates of the opposite party. In 1954, however, the primary law required that the party affiliation of each candidate be printed after his name on the ballot. Thereafter the Democratic party was able to control its own nominations and to present a full ticket of candidates for all offices to the voters at the general election. Before 1954, Democratic nominations were often captured by Republican candidates but Democratic candidates seldom won Republican nominations. The Republican party was better organized and disciplined and followed the practice of selecting its candidates *before* the primary election, thus avoiding intraparty contests. The Democratic victories at the polls in 1958 and subsequent elections indicate that cross filing, while it existed, had greatly aided the better-organized and disciplined Republican party.

What are the prospects of the two major parties in the future? Each party has important assets as well as liabilities. California in all probability will remain a two-party state, despite the unfortunate practice of carving the state into safe legislative districts that hamper interparty competition. A healthy, competitive party system is needed in a state as large and populous as California to represent the varied and multitudinous interests in the state, to provide leadership in the formulation and adoption of important policies and programs, to achieve consensus that is the basis of democratic government, and to make the government truly responsible to the people.

It is a characteristic of a two-party system that the party in office over a period of years accumulates voter grievances against it, real or fancied, and the mistakes it makes and resentments it incurs sooner or later lead to its defeat. The out party gains office when a majority of the voters lose confidence in the party in office. The dynamic character of California's population and economy will undoubtedly facilitate shifts in party control from time to time.

The Democratic party enjoys a lead of nearly 1½ million registered voters, but as events have often witnessed, party registration is an unreliable measure of party strength. In the last four state elections the party has demonstrated its ability to conduct well-organized, strongly financed, effective political campaigns. It usually enjoys the support of organized labor and receives a large majority of the votes of minority groups and persons in the lower-income brackets. Since 1962 the Democratic party has had the advantage of having a large majority of its candidates who were incumbents in office, in particular, legislators who were running for reelection in safe districts. In recent election campaigns the party has been able to put aside its internal differences and form a united front.

The Republican party has strong assets, including the support of the great majority of the press, as well as usually that of business and industry, agriculture, and the professions. Through better organization, more effective campaigns, and attractive candidates it has continued to win elections despite the lead of the Democratic party in the number of registered voters. It has strong financial resources, which are highly important in today's high-cost election campaigns. In recent years right-wing conservative and extremist groups have attempted, sometimes successfully, to wrest control from the moderates who had for many years directed the party organizations and who, as a rule, selected moderates as candidates for public office.

The fortunes of each party will depend in large measure on the quality of its leadership, the qualifications and attractiveness of its candidates, whether the party is united and demonstrates ability to cope wisely with the complex problems of an exploding population, and whether it presents an image that is attractive to the voters.

THE PATTERN OF CALIFORNIA POLITICS

The pattern of politics in California differs from that found in most states. Party organizations and party bosses of the old type have all but disappeared. The great migration of voters into the state and the high mobility of the population in the metropolitan areas does not provide the stable community in which typical party organizations thrive. The adoption of nonpartisan elections for counties as well as cities and other local units has taken away from the party organizations the local contests which provide the basis for "grass-roots" organizations. The extension of the merit system in state and local governments has left few patronage appointments at the disposal of the party in office.

It would be a mistake, however, to assume that California is without politics. On the contrary, it has a highly developed political system, but one which does not follow the old and familiar pattern. With the disappearance of the older type of party organization, whose primary function was to conduct the campaigns for party candidates, other forms of political organization and other types of campaigning have arisen. Campaigns are today waged largely through the media of mass communication —the press, radio, television, billboard, and direct mail. With this change in the form of campaigning and with the breakdown of party functions has come a corresponding change in the location of political power in the state. Candidates no longer owe their election to the efforts of political organizations, but rather to personal campaign organizations. No longer are they elected because of effective precinct work, but rather through well-publicized campaigns. The support of the press, a well-financed campaign, and the support of powerful pressure groups have become much more important to the outcome than the support of party organizations.

The pattern, however, is undergoing change. Despite the long tradition of nonpartisan politics, partisanship is reappearing. Candidates in recent elections, especially Democratic candidates, campaign as partisans and enlist volunteer workers from the party clubs and organizations. Party lines are drawn on many measures before the legislature; party caucuses are regularly held in the Assembly; and the two parties are coming to stand for different policies. Pressure-group politics, which long was the distinctive characteristic of California politics, is being displaced by strengthened political parties and partisan politics.

Several other aspects of California politics are unique. No other state makes as extensive use of the initiative and referendum. Twenty or more propositions are usually put before the voters at the general election, some highly important and bitterly contested, others of little public interest. That the initiative and referendum have worked reasonably well when used so extensively is a source of wonderment. The voters of the state have usually rejected the more radical proposals placed on the ballot. Instead of proving to be a dangerous and radical device, direct legislation has frequently been invoked successfully by conservative interests. As in campaigns for office, the side with the best publicity and press support usually wins.

Another institution widely used in California is the professional public-relations organization which specializes in political campaigns, either for office or on ballot proposals. It has become standard practice for leading candidates to engage public-relations experts to direct their campaigns. This significant development, which is being copied in some other states, is discussed below in greater detail.

Perhaps the most significant aspect of California politics is the rise and development of unofficial party organizations. The California Republican Assembly, founded in 1934 in the face of the rising New Deal tide, proved to be remarkably successful in winning elections for the Republicans. Twenty years later the Democrats followed suit by forming the California Democratic Council, a federation of local Democratic clubs, which take an active part in election campaigns. Both organizations, however, have declined in influence in recent years. The active, real political force today is not found in the official party organizations of either major party, but rather in the unofficial organizations, which are free to select candidates, to endorse them before the primaries, to wage primary and election campaigns for them, and to give meaning and purpose to politics. It is through these organizations rather than the official party organizations that the civic-minded citizen is able to participate in politics.

chapter 2

Political Party Organizations: Official and Unofficial

☆

HOW A POLITICAL PARTY QUALIFIES

How does a political party qualify under state law for a position on the ballot?

A new party must gain a registration of 1 percent of the total number registered or must submit a petition signed by a number of voters equal to 10 percent of the vote cast for governor at the preceding election. After a political party has once qualified, it continues to be recognized as a party as long as one of its candidates for a statewide office receives at least 2 percent of the total vote cast in a gubernatorial election (6 percent if a joint candidate of another party), or if it retains $\frac{1}{15}$ of 1 percent of the total number of voters registered. In 1964, only two political parties met these requirements and appeared on the ballot: Democratic and Republican. The Prohibition party, which had long been on the ballot in California, lost its place after 1962, when it had only 4,824 registered voters and failed to poll 2 percent of the vote cast.

The Communist party was outlawed by an act of the legislature in 1940. This measure was subsequently held unconstitutional by the State Supreme Court, but the party has not qualified since.

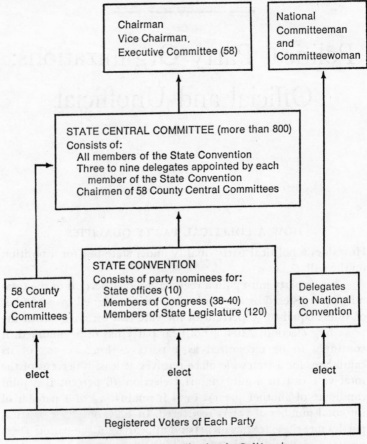

Official Party Organization in California

THE STATE CONVENTION

The state convention, the highest authority of the party, is required by state law to meet at Sacramento every two years following the direct primary election. Under state law each party state convention meets on a Saturday in August following the direct primary. It consists of the nominees of the party for elective state and federal offices, plus holdover incumbents. If any of these persons are not members of the party, the appropriate party committee designates persons to serve in their places. The state convention thus consists of a body of 162 members, including all party candidates for the state legislature and Congress and for statewide offices.

The principal function of the convention is to adopt a platform and, in presidential-election years, to select the party's presidential electors. Before it meets, the state chairman, in consultation with the party leadership, appoints a committee to prepare a preliminary draft of a platform. When the convention meets, the chairman of this group is designated as chairman of the resolutions committee, which consists of a member from each county. Within a few hours this committee approves the platform which has already been prepared, making a few revisions; it is then adopted, usually after only a brief debate, by the convention.

THE STATE CENTRAL COMMITTEE

The state central committee of each party, which is provided for by law, meets once every two years in Sacramento. Instead of being a small governing body of the party, it is a large, unwieldy body of more than 800 persons and exercises only one function—the election of the officers of the party. It meets once, elects the chairman, vice chairman, executive committee, and other officers, then adjourns.

Each member of the state convention is a member of the state central committee and, in addition, appoints three to nine other persons to serve on the committee. The law requires that these members shall be equally divided between men and women. The 58 chairmen of the county central committees are also members of the state central committee.

The state central committee appoints from among its members an executive committee of 58 or more, to which it grants all or a portion of its formal powers. This committee exercises few functions; the actual management of party affairs is entrusted to the party chairman and vice chairman. These offices alternate between the north and the south every two years. For all practical purposes, the party maintains two separate organizations, one for the north and one for the south, which operate quite independently from one another. Although the offices of chairman and vice chairman carry considerable prestige and are usually contested by the leading political personalities and factions within the party, they carry relatively little power and no compensation.

The Democratic party has a steering committee in addition. Created by the state central committee in 1954, this small body serves in an advisory and coordinating capacity, particularly during campaigns. It is composed of national and state party officers and representatives of the California Democratic Council as well as of legislative and congressional candidates. This innovation may well mark the beginning of a long-overdue revision of the party committees in the state.

MEMBERS OF THE NATIONAL PARTY COMMITTEE

The national committeeman and committeewoman of each major party are usually selected by the state delegation to the national convention. The duties of these officials are to aid and advise in the presidential campaign and in the congressional election contests. They take an active part in building the party organization in the state and arranging for national speakers, and are consulted about national patronage, but exercise no authority in the management of state party affairs.

COUNTY CENTRAL COMMITTEE

A county central committee of each party is elected at the direct primary election every two years. It consists usually of from 21 to 30 members, except in Los Angeles County, which has a county central committee exceeding 250 members. Party nominees for the state legislature and holdover legislators are ex officio members of the county central committees.

The county central committees have few functions and, for the most part, play only a minor role in party management. They are not authorized to take any part in the primary elections, and although some county committees have endorsed candidates, this practice has been ruled illegal by the attorney general. Individual members of the committee, however, may support candidates in the primary election and often take an active part. Although given no official voice in the selection of the party nominees, the county central committees are given the function by state law of conducting the election campaigns for the candidates of the party. In actual practice each candidate forms his own campaign committee to supplement the efforts of the county central committee. In the past, the personal campaign organizations of candidates have been more active than the county central committees, but greater use is being made of the latter. The Republican county committees are better organized and financed in most counties than the corresponding Democratic committees, and usually are more active in the campaign.

The county central committee is supposed to maintain a precinct organization throughout the county to get out the voters at elections and to do other campaign work. The job of forming a precinct organization is usually entrusted to a member of the committee, who is designated chairman of the precinct organization. In the larger counties, local chairmen are often appointed in each Assembly district, city, or other local unit. Although each party attempts to form a complete precinct organization before elections, the results usually fall far short of the goal, and the precinct organization virtually disappears between elections.

The activities of the county central committees vary widely from county to county. In the more populous counties they maintain a permanent office and during the campaign are active in arranging political meetings. In some counties the central committees meet regularly, either monthly or quarterly, while in other counties they meet only to organize, and are not called together again except to fill a vacancy for a party nomination which occurs after the direct primary. In most counties there is no contest for the office of county committeeman, and incumbents who have ceased to be active in politics are often reelected. In some counties nominations are rare, the members being elected by the write-in process or appointed. In two small counties no central committees exist in either party.

With such limited functions, the county central committees are relatively ineffective as local party organizations. In some counties it is difficult to get prominent party members to serve. In the larger counties, election to the committee tends to be rather accidental, since the average voter has never heard of the candidates, and often votes for incumbents or those at the top of the list.

It is frequently urged that the county central committees should exercise a more active role in party affairs, but the real center of party activity in most areas has shifted from the official to the unofficial party organizations, a development likely to continue. The unofficial organizations, discussed below, have greater vitality, afford the rank and file of voters greater opportunities for active participation in politics, and, being unofficial, are free to endorse candidates and campaign for them in the primary elections. There is, of course, much cooperation and overlapping of the leadership of the official and unofficial organizations. In areas where the unofficial party organizations are strong they usually dominate the official organization.

OTHER PARTY COMMITTEES

The elections code provides that the executive committee of the state central committee of each party, in conjunction with the nominee of the party for Congress, shall appoint a congressional committee for each district, but such committees are not always appointed and, where they are set up, tend to become merged in the special organization of the candidate to conduct his campaign. On the other hand, although no provision is made in state law for Assembly-district committees, in many districts such organizations exist and often maintain party headquarters and direct the precinct work during the campaign.

From this account it is apparent that the official party organizations are relatively weak and ineffective and do not carry on those activities which are essential to vigorous and healthy party life. For example, they seldom hold conferences or forums for the discussion of public issues and party programs; ordinarily they make little effort to groom potential candidates of the party. Under the nonpartisan type of campaigning in California, they play a relatively minor part in election campaigns.

The weakness of party organizations in California grew from and with the strong nonpartisan tradition which dates from the Progressive era of 1910 to 1920, the public distrust of strong party organization and leadership, and the effort to destroy the boss and machine system. In part, the weakness of official party organization is due to its detailed regulation by state law, which prescribes an inflexible structure, poorly suited to present needs. Witness the anomaly of a state central committee of eight hundred members and virtually no functions! Or the county central committees, elected largely by chance, with few functions and no powers!

In the effort to destroy the boss and machine system, official party organizations were rendered incapable of performing their legitimate functions. The political pattern, however, is changing; partisanship and stronger political organizations are returning to California, though not in the form that generally prevails elsewhere. Many public officers, it should be noted, are lukewarm or even opposed to strong party organizations, official and unofficial. Most elected officers prefer to be free of responsibility to an organized political party, free to decide as they see fit on public issues, although they welcome the aid of party organizations when they are candidates for office. In the absence of effective party organizations candidates for public office generally look to other sources—interest groups, campaign contributors, the party press, lobbyists, organized labor, and other groups—for the support and the means to win primaries and elections. The power wielded by these groups in the state legislature is due to their influence in nominations and elections, and to the relatively weak role of the official party organizations.

The boss and machine of the earlier period have all but

disappeared in California, but new centers of political power have arisen to take their places. The struggle for power continues, for the stakes are high. But the stage has shifted; new actors have appeared on the scene. The pressure group, organized business interests and organized labor, lobbyists and their clients, large campaign contributors, and the press have become the dominant forces in the political struggle. Party organizations have been relegated to a relatively minor part. Campaigns are no longer conducted largely by professional politicians, but today are directed by professional publicity experts.

UNOFFICIAL POLITICAL ORGANIZATIONS

The weakness of official party organizations has led to the establishment of numerous voluntary, unofficial organizations, some of which have formal party ties. Among these are the National Federation of Republican Women, Young Republicans, Young Democrats, United Republicans of California, Republican Associates of Los Angeles, Democratic Associates, Pro-America, Americans for Democratic Action, and others. The last two are not formally identified with one of the major parties, but increasingly Pro-America has become a subsidiary Republican organization, and Americans for Democratic Action generally supports Democratic candidates. There are also various other organizations, some more or less permanent, which spring up during the campaign, many of which exist only on paper or in the imagination of some publicity agent. Organized labor is usually active in political campaigns, working through its own auxiliary organizations.

The two unofficial party organizations of greatest influence in California are the California Republican Assembly and the California Democratic Council. Since 1934, when the California Republican Assembly was formed, it has played a key role in the selection of party candidates, but in recent years its influence has declined and other unofficial Republican organizations have been formed which compete with it. The California Democratic Council, dating only from 1953, has greatly contributed to the rejuvenation and new-found strength of the Democratic party. The development of these statewide unofficial party organizations is another unique feature of California politics. Both have been formed to provide more effective party organization and leadership and to correct weaknesses inherent in the official party machinery and electoral process.

THE CALIFORNIA REPUBLICAN ASSEMBLY

Created in 1934 to promote the interests of the party, the Republican Assembly became in many respects more important and more powerful than the official party organization. There is, it should be noted, little or no conflict between the two organizations. On the contrary, they work in the closest cooperation. Often the same persons are officers in both organizations. The Republican Assembly performs certain functions which the official party organization is not authorized under state law to perform and in other activities works through the regular party machinery.

The founders of the Republican Assembly were a group of insurgents who were dissatisfied with the then conservative, if not reactionary, leadership of the party. Following the defeat of the party in the 1932 election, these young party workers felt the need for a more effective, vigorous party organization and also a new, dynamic program directed at the pressing needs of the state. Within a few years they succeeded in their objective and became the strongest organized force within the ranks of the party.

The major objectives of the California Republican Assembly throughout its history have included the following: (1) to develop a statewide, intelligent, aggressive, and serviceable Republican party; (2) to provide a practical program for the betterment of the party; (3) to further political education and research; and (4) to promote and encourage the activity of its members in politics.

The endorsement and sponsorship of candidates prior to the primary election have been the major functions of the Assembly during its history. The Assemblies throughout the state do not merely wait and see who will enter the race, but are charged with actively seeking out suitable candidates and persuading them to run. The fact that they are able to make assurances to prospective candidates of organized support and adequate financing of the campaign greatly facilitates securing suitable candidates.

The success of the Republican party up to 1958 was due in no small measure to the activities of the Assembly in bringing forward suitable candidates. By endorsing a single candidate for each office the Republican Assembly avoided primary contests between two or more Republican candidates, and was generally able during the period of cross filing to prevent Democratic candidates from capturing Republican nominations for offices. It also avoided bitter intraparty contests which weaken the party in the final election.

The local Assembly chapters participate actively in primary and election campaigns, cooperating with other Republican groups and the official organization. One of its most important activities is the formation of a United Finance Committee in each county to solicit funds to support Republican candidates. Through this arrangement the Assembly is able to assure potential candidates of adequate financial support, a consideration of utmost importance in persuading leading citizens to be candidates for public office.

Until recent years the Assembly was not identified with either the conservative or liberal wing of the party, but was a unifying force, recruiting and supporting candidates who would appeal broadly to all factions. Under increasing pressure from right-wing groups, however, it has moved to the right and declined to endorse Senator Thomas Kuchel in 1962, who went on to win by a large majority in the election. In 1964 the right wing captured control of the Assembly in a stormy session which endorsed Goldwater for President by a large majority. "Ultra Right Rules the GOP" was the headline of a *San Francisco Chronicle* account of the convention. Joseph Martin, Jr., former Republican National Committeeman from California, declared that the Assembly no longer represented a cross section of the party. The Assembly has lost much of its former influence and no longer speaks for the party as a whole.

THE CALIFORNIA DEMOCRATIC COUNCIL

It took the Democrats nearly twenty years to follow the example of the Republicans in setting up an effective unofficial party organization, but when the California Democratic Council was formed in 1953 it quickly became a potent force in California politics.

The California Democratic Council is a federation of some 500 local clubs throughout the state with an estimated 60,000 paying members. Democratic attempts to set up auxiliary organizations to strengthen the party and win their own nominations date from the early 1940s, but it was not until 1952, with the impetus afforded by the popularity of the Democratic candidate, Adlai Stevenson, that the club movement succeeded. These clubs survived the Democratic defeat of that year and continued as forums for discussion of public issues and avenues of political activities.

Many Democratic leaders welcomed the clubs as a grass-roots movement which might be utilized to strengthen the party and provide volunteer workers in campaigns. In 1953 the local clubs were merged into a statewide organization, the California Democratic Council (CDC). Local clubs are formed into Assembly-district and congressional-district councils. A formal tie-in with the official party organization is achieved by the provision that local clubs may be chartered only by the county central committees of the party; the Assembly-district and congressional-district councils are chartered by and responsible to the CDC. At the top of the organizational pyramid is the annual CDC convention, composed of approximately 2,000 delegates. This body elects CDC officers, discusses issues, passes resolutions, and in election years endorses candidates for the Democratic nomination for statewide offices.

Although the major function of the CDC and its local councils, like that of the Republican Assemblies, is to endorse candidates prior to the primary election, and although the local clubs ring doorbells, solicit funds, and otherwise take a leading part in political campaigns, it would be a mistake to assume that this is their only activity. The clubs carry on a year-round program of forums, panel discussions, and social activities. Prominent speakers are invited to address them on timely subjects, often unrelated to politics. Without clubhouses, they meet in school buildings and the homes of members. These year-round activities are extremely important, for without them the clubs would not be able to maintain their membership and keep up the interest of members. When an election approaches, the clubs turn their attention to political matters: the selection of candidates, the soliciting of campaign funds, and active campaigning.

The membership of the clubs is heavily weighted with persons from the middle classes, business and professional people and their wives, mostly university graduates, and hence is not representative of the rank and file of the party. The clubs thrive in middle-class residential areas but languish in the older urban districts and sections populated by blue-collar workers. Members are definitely "eggheads," liberally oriented, interested in public affairs and wanting to do something about them. They are a unique phenomenon in American politics—a nonpatronage political club of voters who are ready to volunteer their services without hope of reward. Doubtless many of the leaders are politically ambitious and look upon club work as a ladder to a public career, but the rank and file join for the satisfaction of participation in politics, the advancement of a cause or ideal.

The success of the Democratic party since 1954 may be attributed in considerable part to the endorsement of candidates by the CDC and to the work of the Democratic clubs in the campaign, whose members have carried the brunt of doorbell-ringing in the precincts. Despite this success, a number of prominent Democrats view the clubs with misgivings, fearing that they may abuse their new-found power. Democratic legislators resent the attempts by some of the clubs to dictate their votes on key measures, and especially attacks on their records by the clubs. The legislator feels that he is much better informed on highly complex legislative bills than the club members, and, moreover, is responsible to all of the voters in his district.

A struggle for power between the Democratic "pros" and the CDC "amateurs" which may disrupt party unity in future elections appears to be in the offing, although so far the pros and the amateurs have been able to put aside their differences and work together in election campaigns. Critics maintain that the CDC has been taken over by left wingers and persons who wish to use it for their own purposes and that it no longer represents the rank and file of the party. Only time will tell whether the Democratic clubs will survive and continue to be an effective force in the politics of the state. Similar movements in the past have usually disappeared after a few years, especially after suffering defeat, or have been taken over by professional politicians and have lost their crusading zeal. A weakness of unofficial party organizations is that they may be taken over by extremists and used to promote policies and programs which do not have the approval of the rank and file of party voters.

chapter 3

Nominations and Elections

☆

TYPES OF ELECTIONS

General elections are held on the first Tuesday after the first Monday of November in even-numbered years. In presidential-election years the voters elect not only the state's presidential electors for President and Vice President, but also members of Congress, a United States Senator when a term expires, members of the state Assembly, and half of the members of the state Senate. Judges and special-district officers are also elected at the same election on a nonpartisan ballot. In alternate even-numbered years the governor and other state officers, members of Congress, and members of the state legislature are elected on a partisan ballot, while county and other local officers and judges are elected on a nonpartisan ballot. Initiative and referendum propositions may be voted on at each election. Direct primary elections for the nomination of the candidates of each party for partisan offices are held on the first Tuesday in June of even-numbered years. At the primary elections registered voters of each party elect the members of the county central committees.

Delegates to the national party conventions are elected at the direct primary preceding the conventions.

Municipal elections, which are nonpartisan, are held ordinarily in the spring of odd-numbered years at the times specified by city charters or state law. In some cities they are preceded by nonpartisan primaries, the purpose of which is to eliminate all but the two highest candidates for each office. Candidates who poll a majority of all votes cast for the office in the nonpartisan primary are usually declared elected. Many cities do not use a nonpartisan primary before municipal elections. In these cities the candidates who receive the highest vote, or a plurality, are declared elected. Special elections are called from time to time to fill vacancies or to vote on special issues or the recall of public officers.

All in all, the California voter has a heavy and responsible task of choosing among scores of candidates for state and local offices and voting on numerous propositions. That he is able to make reasonably intelligent choices is a tribute to his civic interest and judgment, but it must be admitted that the large majority of voters are relatively uninformed about the qualifications of many candidates and the merits of numerous propositions on which they have to vote, and rely on the recommendations of political parties, the press, various organizations, and friends.

QUALIFICATIONS FOR VOTING

The state constitution requires the voter to be: (1) a citizen of the United States for at least 90 days; (2) 21 years of age; (3) a resident of the state for one year, of the county for 90 days, and of the precinct for 54 days; and (4) able to read the constitution and to sign his name, unless physically unable to do so. Since the 1960 election, new residents may vote for President, but not for any other office, after only 54 days in the state.

Voters are required to register at least 53 days before the election. If a voter changes his residence after the close of registration, he may vote from his previous address at the following election. Registration is conducted by the county clerk (registrar of voters in Los Angeles, San Francisco and several other large counties), and by persons appointed by him as registration deputies. Usually the city clerk of each city is authorized to register voters. Registration is permanent as long as the voter continues to reside at the same address and votes at least once every two years.

A voter who is absent from his legal residence may register by applying by mail to the county clerk or registrar of voters of his county. After receipt of the necessary forms and instructions he must appear before an officer authorized to administer oaths to complete the absentee registration. The voter must state his party affiliation when he registers in order to qualify to vote for party nominations in the primary election. Those who decline to so state are permitted to vote only for nonpartisan offices and measures in the primary election. In 1966 more than 200,000 voters declined to state a party affiliation and thus were deprived of the right to vote in the direct primary election of either party.

NOMINATION OF CANDIDATES: DIRECT PRIMARY ELECTIONS

The nomination of candidates for public office is the key function of political parties in a democracy. Each political party seeks to secure control of the government and to wield the power of office by electing its candidates to executive and legislative offices. Each bids for public support in two ways: (1) by adopting platforms and resolutions stating its principles, policies, and proposed programs (and denouncing the opposing party); and (2) by nominating candidates whom it strives to elect. Of these two, the nomination of candidates is by far the more important. Political platforms are usually filled with glittering generalities, clichés, platitudes, and "weasel" pronouncements that are designed to mean all things to all men. Fearing to offend important groups of voters, parties seldom take stands in their platforms on controversial issues. Few voters bother to read the platforms, and with good reason.

It is by the candidates whom they nominate for public offices that political parties indicate the principles, policies, and programs that they support, and if elected to office will attempt to put into effect. When a party nominates a candidate for public office, it, in effect, certifies him to the voters as a citizen who is well qualified for the office and one who may be relied on to support the principles and policies of the party. Obviously the manner in which each party selects its candidates is of the utmost importance. Well-qualified citizens who are successful in their chosen professions, occupations, or businesses seldom spontaneously seek public office at great expense and personal sacrifice. Unless the party has some means, formal or informal, to seek out qualified citizens and encourage them to stand for office by assuring them of support, the race is left to self-announcers, persons often of mediocre qualifications who seek the prominence and possibly the personal gain to be secured through election to public office.

California has tried out various nominating systems, none of which has been entirely successful. Party conventions were generally used before the first law making direct primary elections mandatory was adopted in 1909. Delegates to the conventions were notoriously boss- and machine-controlled, and the conventions became thoroughly discredited as undemocratic and often corrupt. The direct-primary law was modified in 1913 by an amendment which permitted candidates to enter the primaries of any or all political parties, or to cross file, which greatly changed the character of the primary elections. As cross filing became the accepted practice, the primary elections became, in fact though not in form, the final election for most offices, the winning candidate securing the nominations of both major political parties.

The merits and demerits of cross filing were debated for years. The operation of the plan was vitally changed after 1952 by the provision requiring the party designations of candidates to be printed on the primary ballots. Thereafter it was much more difficult for a Democrat to capture the Republican nomination, and vice versa, and both parties were able for the first time in years to present virtually full slates of candidates to the voters in the final election. Finally, in 1959, cross filing was eliminated entirely by the Democratic legislature. Its elimination was one of the first items on the agenda of the Democrats when the legislature met, and was accomplished despite the fact that many legislators of both parties favored cross filing inasmuch as it greatly aided incumbents toward being reelected.

The ending of cross filing gave each party the power to nominate its own candidates for each elective partisan office. With few exceptions, therefore, all offices are contested in the general election, providing the voter in the general election with a choice. This option is in great contrast to the practice under cross filing, when in the majority of contests the winning candidate in the primary captured the nomination of both parties and hence was unopposed in the general election. The ending of cross filing has brought about a great increase in intraparty primary contests as well as interparty contests in the general election. Election campaigns have become more partisan; candidates of both parties tend to take more definite stands upon important state issues, although many public policies are outside the area of party controversy. The legislature, especially the Assembly, has become more partisan since the elimination of cross filing. Members of each party in the Assembly regularly meet in caucus, and votes on many social, economic, welfare, labor, and public-finance measures follow party lines. Whether this change is for the better may be debated, but it is probably here to stay.

In the absence of cross filing the parties are no longer in danger of losing nominations to the opposite party; nevertheless, the unofficial party organizations in both parties continue to endorse candidates before the primary. Their endorsements, however, carry less weight than formerly; many candidates in each party run for its nomination without endorsement and at times defeat the endorsed candidate. Preprimary endorsement of candidates by an unofficial party organization has been criticized on the ground that under the direct primary it is the function of the voters rather than of a small, self-selected, and often unrepresentative group of party activists to choose the nominees of the party. It is attacked as undemocratic and subject to abuse by persons or groups who may capture control of the unofficial party organization and wield this power for selfish interests. Another criticism is that preprimary endorsements of candidates by a group claiming to speak for the party interfere with the right of citizens to be candidates for public office. Several bills have been introduced in recent years to prohibit preprimary endorsements, but have not come to a vote in the legislature.

The preprimary endorsement of candidates by an unofficial party organization effects some purposes of the former party-convention method of nominating candidates within the procedural framework of the direct primary, which is almost universally used today. The unofficial party organization acts as a screening committee which reviews the qualifications, suitability, and electability of the candidates, and judges whether they are in agreement with the accepted principles of the party. If necessary, it may seek out qualified candidates to enter the race. The unofficial party organization can only endorse the candidates whom it selects; the final choice of nominees rests with the voters of the party. The voters, however, usually have little reliable information about the qualifications of the many candidates and necessarily must rely largely upon the recommendation of party leaders, statements by the party press, and endorsements by various unofficial party organizations and other groups. The CRA and the CDC no longer have a monopoly in endorsing candidates; other party groups, organized labor, and other organizations also make preprimary endorsements, and the voter can take his choice.

In primary elections today the voter is called upon to choose among fifty or more candidates, as a rule, for about twenty-five different offices, partisan and nonpartisan. The large number of candidates makes his task of choosing wisely a difficult or impossible one without some guidance. The number of candidates has greatly increased in recent years. No longer are potential candidates reluctant to enter the primary without the endorsement of the CRA or CDC. In 1966, an all-time high of 788 candidates entered the party primaries for the 120 state legislative seats, the 38 seats in Congress, and the four memberships on the state Board of Equalization; 47 candidates ran for the six partisan statewide offices and one nonpartisan office. Very few offices were uncontested. In almost all instances the voters were given a choice, but unfortunately it was often among poorly qualified or unattractive candidates.

Any citizen who has the prescribed qualifications for an office may become a candidate for the nomination of his party by filing a declaration of his candidacy, accompanied by a nominating petition signed by from 20 to 100 qualified voters, who are called sponsors, and by posting the required fee. The required filing fee for state officers and members of Congress is 2 percent of the annual salary of the office, while that for the members of the state legislature is $20 and for county offices $10.

The candidate who receives the highest vote in each party primary wins the nomination of the party. In the event that a vacancy in the nomination of a party occurs at least 40 days before the election, the appropriate party committee is authorized to designate another person as the party's nominee.

THE PRESIDENTIAL PREFERENCE PRIMARY

California is one of approximately fifteen states which hold a presidential preference primary every four years to permit voters to express their preference for the party's nominee for President and to elect delegates to the national party convention. The other states elect their delegates to the national convention by means of party conventions, at which the delegates may or may not be instructed to vote for a favored candidate. The California presidential primary, which is held in the first week of June every four years, is the last primary before the conventions meet; because of the large bloc of votes which the state holds, the results of California's primary often are a decisive factor in the choice of the party's nominee. The Goldwater victory in the California primary in 1964 virtually assured his nomination.

California voters express their choice of the nominee for President by voting for a group of delegates who are pledged to that candidate. The delegates are elected as a group; their names do not appear on the ballot—only the name of the candidate to whom they are pledged. If a group enters the primary without expressing a preference for the presidential nominee, as was done in 1964 when President Johnson declined to permit his name to be used, the name of the chairman of the group is printed on the ballot with the heading "Candidates expressing no preference." To qualify for a place on the ballot, a group of candidates for delegates to the national party convention must submit a petition signed by 1 percent of the number of voters for the party's gubernatorial candidate at the preceding election.

The national convention is the big show of the party, where its great and near great assemble every four years to reiterate their faith and allegiance, to renew old friendships and make new ones, to hear party orators praise the party's record to the skies and excoriate the record of the opposing party, and to nominate the party candidates for President and Vice President, to whom (almost) all pledge their allegiance. Its proceedings are conducted amid noise, confusion, and pandemonium. Yet it usually selects candidates wisely, picking those who are most electable if not always those who are best qualified. In 1964, however, the Republican national convention departed from its usual practice of selecting its candidates from the center and nominated Barry Goldwater from the right wing, a candidate whose overwhelming defeat was already indicated by the public-opinion polls. Last-minute efforts were made by Governor Scranton of Pennsylvania and others to head off the nomination of Senator Goldwater, which they realized would result in disastrous defeat for the party, but it was too late. They had relied too long on Governor Nelson Rockefeller to collect enough delegates to block Goldwater's nomination, but Rockefeller was unacceptable to the majority of the Republican voters because of his liberal views and his recent divorce.

The leading members of each party, including those holding

high political office, former candidates, members of the United States Senate and House of Representatives, members of the state legislature, party officials, large contributors, and others eagerly seek the honor and recognition of being a member of the delegation to the national convention. Although California has a large delegation—80 with one vote each to the 1964 Republican national convention and 160 with half votes to the Democratic convention—there are never enough places to meet the demand. Those who are disappointed may be given a consolation prize by being appointed as alternate delegates. Each delegate and alternate must pay for his own travel and expenses, which may amount to a thousand dollars or more.

The California presidential preference primary has been criticized because the winning candidate captures the entire state delegation and its large bloc of votes in the convention. The entire vote of the state in the national convention may thus turn on a few thousand votes in a close primary race, and the delegation sent to the convention may not reflect the true will of the party voters. In 1964 Goldwater won the Republican primary with less than 52 percent of the total vote, carrying only 14 counties. Rockefeller carried 44 counties, with large majorities in many northern counties, but did not receive a single vote from California in the convention. The Goldwater delegation, which was made up of right-wing conservative Republicans who would stick with him if the convention became deadlocked, included few leading Republican office holders. The delegation voted solidly against several proposals to liberalize the platform, leading the *San Francisco Chronicle* to criticize it as unrepresentative of the great body of moderate and liberal Republican voters in the state. The exclusion of moderates and liberals from the delegation increased the difficulties of the party in healing its wounds from the primary contest and achieving the party unity and harmony that are essential to success in the election.

Two groups of candidates for delegates to the national convention entered the Democratic presidential primary in 1964, each group expressing no preference of candidates, since President Johnson declined to permit his name to be entered. One group, headed by Governor Brown, polled over two-thirds of the vote cast; the second group, entered by an opposing faction within the party, was headed by Mayor Samuel Yorty of Los Angeles.

CAMPAIGN STRATEGY AND TACTICS

"As in the past," announced Governor Earl Warren in opening his campaign for reelection in 1950, "I will submit my candidacy to the people of both parties. I will make no appeal to . . . partisanship . . . I will not permit myself to be encumbered by any entrenched political machine." It has been common practice in the past for candidates of both major political parties to conduct nonpartisan campaigns for state and national offices and to place little reliance upon the party organizations.

Political campaigning in California, however, has greatly changed in recent years. Partisanship returned to election campaigns after changes were made in the primary law that enabled each party to present a full slate of candidates to the voters in the final election, and because of the rise of the party clubs. The little designations "Dem" and "Rep" on the primary ballots after the names of candidates in 1954 made a great difference in the appeals used by candidates. Democratic candidates desiring to capitalize on the heavy party registration in most districts began to run as Democrats instead of as nonpartisans. Republican candidates, usually facing the necessity of winning the votes of Democrats as well as Republicans, continue to use nonpartisan as well as partisan appeals. This change in campaign strategy marks a revolution in California politics, where formerly candidates of all parties usually ran as nonpartisans.

Much of the campaigning in California is designed to publicize the candidate rather than the ticket or the party, although in recent campaigns the California Democratic Council distributed throughout the state mailing pieces urging the election of the entire party slate. For the most part candidates conduct highly personal campaigns, utilizing a personal organization of campaign managers and committees. Individual members of the state central committee or the county central committees are often active in the campaign of particular candidates, but in the past the role played by the official party organizations has been much smaller than that of the corresponding party organizations in other states.

Candidates for the lesser offices often seek election "on the coat-tails" of a popular leading candidate. Thus in 1958 the Democratic candidates generally associated themselves with the popular candidate for governor, Edmund G. (Pat) Brown, and in many instances were able to ride his coat-tails to victory. The opposite tactic was used by Republican candidates in the same campaign. After the poor showing of Senator Knowland in the primary and because of his stand on the "right to work" initiative, which alienated the labor vote, many Republican candidates sought to disassociate their campaigns from that of the head of the ticket.

Candidates for statewide offices usually set up twin organizations to conduct their campaigns, one for northern California and another for the southern part of the state. Each part operates quite independently of the other, as a rule, with its own set of campaign managers, speakers' bureaus, and local chairmen, co-chairmen, and committees. Often the person designated as campaign manager of an area or committee chairman is chosen largely for his prestige, while the active campaign work is in the hands of a paid expert or public-relations firm.

The use of professional publicity firms is standard practice in all well-financed statewide campaigns. Since campaigning largely consists of publicizing the candidate, this is entirely understandable. Some professional campaign organizations manage all aspects of the campaign. They write the speeches of the candidate, schedule events which will secure favorable publicity, arrange public meetings, select local campaign committees, and turn out publicity releases almost daily. The cost of their services is high, as, indeed, is the cost of campaigning for office in California.

These firms are highly skilled in planning and conducting campaigns, in building up candidates as appealing personalities or in manufacturing public opinion in favor of or opposed to a given measure. They are artists in the use of the slogan and the campaign cliché, in the use of colorful, fighting, appealing prose, and in the manipulation of mass appeals. They are experts in judging what appeals will go over with the public, and they not only publicize what the candidate has said but also tell him what to say. For a fee, they are prepared to sell a candidate or an issue to the public, in much the same manner as an automobile, refrigerator, or soap may be sold, utilizing all of the techniques of modern advertising.

The most widely known political public-relations firm is that of Whitaker and Baxter in San Francisco. They managed the campaigns of Warren in 1942 and Knight in 1954 and have conducted many campaigns for or against ballot measures with remarkable success. They were also retained by the American Medical Association to carry on a nationwide campaign against compulsory health insurance. Other campaign-management firms include Harry Lerner and Associates of San Francisco, and Baus and Ross Company, Elwood J. Robinson, Stephen L. Wells Company, and Keene and Associates, all of Los Angeles. Joseph A. Robinson Associates of San Francisco specializes in circulating petitions designed to secure the signatures required for placing initiative and referendum measures on the ballot, occasionally qualifying conflicting propositions for the same election.

The major effort in most political campaigns is to bring the candidate to the attention of the voters, to build him up as a public figure, with an appealing personality, a smiling face, and an attractive family. Invariably he is pictured as a man of sterling character, a paragon of wisdom and virtue, deeply interested in the public welfare. But most effort is devoted simply to registering his name and face in the public mind with a slogan that epitomizes what he is supposed to stand for.

California elections have at times been marred by dirty political campaigning. Campaign managers attempt to create a favorable image of the candidate in the mind of the voters and an unfavorable image of the opposing candidate. Personal attacks on an opponent, however, must be made with care or they will be resented by many voters and may backfire. Often they consist of rumors, innuendos, and insinuations rather than direct accusations, and are spread by a whispering campaign or by anonymous publications issued in the closing days of the campaign when there is insufficient time to answer them. Incumbents in office are often attacked indirectly by accusing their assistants or appointees of incompetence or misconduct in office.

In close contests each side is tempted to resort to questionable appeals, unsupported charges, and even downright misrepresentations in a desperate attempt to win additional votes needed to assure election. The opposing candidate may be portrayed as a dangerous radical, associated with dangerous left-wing groups, or "soft on communism"; or he may be pictured as a mossback reactionary, the tool of special interests, and associated with extreme right-wing and fascist groups. In some areas appeals based on racial or religious bigotry are often used.

The bitterly fought campaign for governor in 1962 was notable for the vicious attacks on both candidates and those associated with them through misrepresentations, smears, bogus charges, doctored pictures, and campaign publicity issued by anonymous and fictitious organizations. Leading members of both parties and the executive director of the national Fair Campaign Practices Committee termed the campaign the dirtiest on record. Three campaign pamphlets issued by fictitious sponsors and subsequently disavowed by the party organization were banned by a court order because of scurrilous and defamatory charges, misrepresentations, doctored pictures, and violations of campaign-practices laws requiring the publication of the names of persons or organizations issuing campaign materials.

Two of the banned pamphlets contained doctored pictures of Governor Brown. One pictured him bowing deferentially to Khrushchev and quoted Brown as saying: "Premier Khrushchev, we who admire you, who respect you, welcome you to California." Brown denied making any such statement. The picture of him had been cropped from a photograph of Brown being introduced to an oriental visitor. Another picture of Brown, which presumably showed him cheering a CDC resolution urging the recognition of Communist China, had been taken from a photograph of him cheering a polio-crippled child.

The third pamphlet banned by court order was in the form of a questionnaire addressed to Democratic voters, but was in reality a vicious attack on the CDC as a left-wing, procommunist organization. The questionnaire had been issued by the "Committee for the Preservation of the Democratic Party," but on inquiry it was discovered that there was no such committee, and it was unknown at the address listed. The use of fictitious committees with high-sounding titles, preferably nonpartisan, is an old campaign trick to catch the unwary.

In the 1962 election campaign the Democrats circulated widely a several-years-old report accusing Nixon while Vice President of arranging a loan to his mother and brother by Howard Hughes, a prominent Los Angeles industrialist, who had received large government contracts. Nixon vehemently denied the accusation and in a debate with Brown challenged him to make the charge publicly. Nixon also accused the Democrats of circulating lies about his stands on right-to-work laws, social security, and civil rights, and attempting to frighten workers, the aged, and minority groups into voting against him.

THE HIGH COST OF POLITICAL CAMPAIGNS [1]

Few citizens are aware of how much it costs to mount an effective political campaign in California for a major statewide office. In the primary campaign, 3 to 5 million party voters must be reached; in the general-election campaign, more than 8 million. The official reports of campaign expenditures filed by the candi-

---

[1] For a discussion of campaign finance, see: Alexander Heard, *The Costs of Democracy* (Chapel Hill: University of North Carolina Press, 1960) ; *Financing Presidential Campaigns,* Report of the President's Commission on Campaign Costs, 1962; Herbert E. Alexander and Laura L. Denny, *Regulation of Political Finance* (Berkeley: Institute of Government Studies, University of California, 1966).

dates and their campaign committees after elections are far from complete and do not include expenditures on behalf of the candidate made by other organizations such as unofficial party organizations and committees and other bodies active in the campaign. These organizations are not required to report their expenditures.

Consequently there are no accurate and complete statistics on campaign costs, but only incomplete reports and unofficial estimates. One of the most effective ways of concealing the amounts being spent in a campaign is to utilize numerous committees, each operating largely independently of the others and raising its own funds. Unfortunately, federal and state laws permit and encourage the use of a multiplicity of committees and other organizations in political campaigns, thus defeating any effective centralized control and responsibility.

In the Brown-Nixon race for governor in 1962 the campaign committees of each candidate reported expenditure of approximately $500,000 in the primary campaign and $1½ million in the general-election campaign—a total expenditure of approximately $2 million for each candidate. If we allow for unreported expenditures in behalf of each candidate by unofficial party organizations and committees and for the candidates' shares of the expenditures of the official party organizations, the total expenditures of both candidates would exceed $5 million.

The campaign expenditures in the 1964 Democratic primary of the two leading candidates for the nomination for the United State Senate afford striking evidence of the high cost of campaigning in California, as well as the problems and difficulties in conducting a campaign to inform 5 million party voters about the candidates and issues. The campaign committee of one candidate, State Controller Alan Cranston, filed a report of its expenditures totaling $823,407, which, it may be noted, considerably exceeded its receipts. After his defeat by Pierre Salinger, Cranston wrote an illuminating article on campaign expenditures, which was published in *Fortune*.[2]

---

[2] November, 1964, p. 124. The following account draws heavily on this article.

Cranston estimated that the total expenditures in his behalf, including those of other organizations which were not reported, were approximately $1 million. Salinger's campaign committee reported an expenditure of $481,000, but Cranston estimated that expenditures for Salinger, including those made by other groups, would also be approximately $1 million. This expenditure by each candidate of about 20 cents per voter for the nearly 5 million registered Democrats does not appear to be excessive. It may be noted that a single mailing to the Democratic voters would have cost $250,000 for postage alone if sent by first-class mail; the total cost of a single mailing to all Democratic voters, including printing, addressing, stuffing envelopes, and the like, would probably have been twice this amount.

Cranston pointed out in the *Fortune* article that most expenditures in political campaigns are designed primarily to project the image of the candidate that his campaign managers believe will appeal to voters rather than to convey a message about his qualifications and stands on public issues. His committee spent $95,957 for billboards, which are necessarily limited to the name and picture of the candidate and a slogan consisting of one or two words, such as "EXPERIENCED" or "INTEGRITY," which is all that the speeding motorist has time to read. Television and radio, on which $250,000 was spent, presented the same problem. The two candidates conducted an hour-long debate in which they were able to discuss the issues and express their ideas and convictions, and viewers were able to make a subjective evaluation of what kind of person each candidate was, but quite likely their viewers consisted almost entirely of voters who had already made up their minds about the candidates, in which event the debate did not enable the candidates to reach undecided voters. Most television and radio funds were spent for ten-second spot announcements, which in fact were only six seconds long, allowing for a one-second interval before and after and for the statement labeling the paid political announcement. A six-second announcement, which on a major television station in prime hours costs $800, allowed time only for the photograph of the candidate and the briefest possible message. A longer announcement would have permitted a more meaningful message at a correspondingly higher cost, but had the disadvantage that it would have allowed time for voters to turn to another channel.

Advertisements in the press provide a more suitable medium in political campaigns to reach voters with a meaningful appeal, but here too the message must be brief if it is to be widely read. Select mailings, on which Cranston's committee spent $204,000, were used in preference to a mailing to all Democratic voters, which was deemed to be too expensive. A favored method of campaigning today is for the candidate to meet and shake hands with voters, but only a few hundred among five million voters can be reached in this manner.

The 1964 Cranston-Salinger primary campaign for the nomination for United States senator indicates that even a million dollars is insufficient for conducting an effective campaign for one of the two leading political offices in the state and for informing the voters about the candidates and the issues. The cost of a general-election campaign, which is almost always contested, is ordinarily twice as great as that of a primary campaign.

The primary-campaign costs of candidates for other statewide offices are considerably smaller than those of candidates for governor and United States senator, but even these usually involved expenditures of several hundred thousand dollars. Afterward, the winning candidate in the primary faces the need to raise even larger funds for the general-election campaign. He is not able to rely on the party organization to conduct this campaign for him, as it does in some states; instead, he must conduct a separate campaign to supplement the campaign activities of the regular party organization. A contested primary campaign for member of Congress will usually cost the leading candidates from $25,000 to $50,000 or even more, and the general-election campaign for candidates who win the primary elections may be considerably more costly. Congressional districts today have an average population of nearly a half million and more than 200,000 registered voters. The campaign expenditures of candidates for the state Assembly usually run about half what must be spent by a candidate for Congress, but vary widely depending upon whether the candidate is an incumbent and whether the district is safe or closely contested.

The most serious effect of the high cost of political campaigns is that persons elected to high public offices are placed under heavy obligation toward those who have financed their campaigns. The candidate with the largest campaign fund does not always win, but the candidate who is judged the likely winner has the least difficulty in raising campaign funds. Large contributors are reluctant to contribute to a losing candidate who will be unable to repay their generosity with appropriate reward or recognition.

Aware that "he who pays the piper calls the tune," prominent citizens of the highest integrity often refuse to become candidates for public office, knowing or at least fearing that they will be placed under heavy obligation to those who have financed their campaign even though they make no commitment to campaign contributors. The large campaign contributor normally expects access to the legislator or public official whom he has helped to elect; indeed, not merely access but the active assistance of the official in securing desired action by the government. Large contributors often expect and demand a *quid pro quo* for their contribution; others who do not exact any promise of the candidate contribute only to candidates whom they are sure will vote "right" on measures affecting the contributor. Organized labor gives its financial assistance to candidates who agree to support labor's position on legislative measures.

Candidates for public office, as a rule, are politically ambitious and seek to achieve a political career that will provide them with ego satisfaction, power, prestige, public recognition, and opportunity for public service. Only persons who are strongly motivated are prepared to incur the risks that are involved and to make the personal sacrifices required of those who seek public office. To achieve his ambition the candidate must have strong financial backing. Large campaign contributors are thus able to wield strong influences on government policies and often receive favored treatment at the expense of the taxpayer and the public.

Yet it would be a serious mistake to assume that all campaign contributors demand a *quid pro quo* for their contributions. Many persons of wealth, without expecting favors in return, contribute to the campaigns of candidates whom they regard as capable and who have "sound" ideas and principles about government. Business and industrial leaders often take the initiative in recruiting suitable candidates for public office and undertake to raise the necessary campaign funds from among their associates without exacting any commitment from the candidate, with the expectation even so that he will follow policies that are agreeable to his backers.

The objectionable effects of campaign contributions would be obviated if campaign funds were donated by many small contributors instead of by a few large contributors. But attempts to raise campaign funds through small contributions by the rank and file of voters have generally been unsuccessful. Low-income voters, as a rule, are unwilling to contribute to political campaigns; middle-income voters are seldom sufficiently motivated to make more than a nominal contribution. Consequently, the bulk of campaign funds are contributed by wealthy persons, many of whom desire influence and power and wish to protect vested interests or secure favorable governmental policies.

In California, as in other states, the largest contributions to political campaigns are made by business and industrial leaders, especially leaders in activities subject to government regulation and requiring government protection, and by organized labor. Some business firms contribute to both parties in order to have friends in both camps. Business interests generally contribute to the Republican party and to conservative candidates of both parties, while organized labor contributes principally to Democratic candidates and to Republican candidates who support labor. Although federal laws prohibit corporations and labor unions from contributing to political campaigns, various loopholes are utilized to get around this prohibition.

The High Cost of Campaigns · 73

Political parties and individual candidates make extensive use of dinners as a means of raising campaign funds. The price per plate ranges from $10 to $1,000, depending upon the occasion. Campaign fund-raising dinners amount to a thinly veiled assessment of office holders, lobbyists, government contractors, business firms, labor unions, and others who for one reason or another feel obligated to attend or at least to purchase tickets. In defense of this method of soliciting campaign contributions, it may be said that such political dinners increase the number of campaign contributors and lessen the dependence upon large contributors. Public officials and employees who are outside of the civil service are often assessed a percentage of their salary as a campaign contribution, which they must pay or incur the risk of losing their jobs.

State as well as federal laws regulating campaign expenditures are notoriously ineffective. It is seldom that any attempt whatever is made to enforce them. The maximum limits placed on campaign expenditures in most states are absurdly low, virtually forcing candidates and their campaign committees to violate the law and to find various ways of spending money in the campaign without having to report it. Because of the dissatisfaction with the former arbitrary limits placed on campaign expenditures, the California legislature several years ago repealed all limits on the amounts that may be spent, relying instead on public reporting of campaign expenditures to act as a deterrent against excessive expenditures. The law, however, has not had the desired effect, for only the candidate and his campaign committee are required to report their expenditures. Other committees and organizations are not required to report. Even the reports of the candidate and his campaign committee are not required until 35 days after the election, when there is no longer any active interest in campaign expenditures. If public reporting of campaign expenditures is to have a salutary effect, reports must be made during the campaign rather than a month afterwards, and must include all expenditures.

A reform often proposed is to require each candidate to

appoint a campaign manager who is solely responsible for all expenditures made in his behalf, other than those made by the party organization in the election campaign, and to prohibit any campaign expenditure by others. This feature is central in the British law regulating campaign expenditures, and was recently enacted into law by the Florida legislature. Centralization of responsibility and control over campaign expenditures is necessary in order to enforce state regulations and to assure accurate and complete financial reports.

Another proposal, for government to subsidize political parties and thus bear part of the cost of political campaigns, was advocated by President Theodore Roosevelt in 1907. Several bills providing for a government subsidy to political parties in proportion to their number of registered voters have been introduced in recent sessions of the California legislature. The states of Oregon and North Dakota subsidize political campaigns by issuing a voters' handbook, which is mailed to all registered voters. By paying a nominal fee, the candidate receives a page in the handbook, which usually includes his photograph, biography, and statement of his platform. Several California cities issue a similar handbook to voters before municipal elections. A voters' handbook gives every candidate access to the electorate for a nominal cost and thus reduces but does not eliminate the necessity for each candidate to conduct a campaign to publicize his qualifications and stands on public issues.

The late President Kennedy, recognizing the importance of campaign finance, appointed a presidential commission of persons from both political parties to study the problem of financing presidential campaigns and to submit recommendations. Its major recommendations included the following: (1) that citizens and private organizations as a civic responsibility help finance *bipartisan* political activities to assist both political parties in informing voters about candidates and issues; (2) that tax incentives be provided to encourage citizen contributions to the party or candidate of their choice; (3) that limits on campaign expenditures be abolished and full and complete disclosure of campaign expenditures be made during the campaign. The commission did not recommend government subsidy of campaign expenditures, but did recommend continuing study of the problem of campaign finance. California and Minnesota have enacted legislation permitting campaign contributions to be deducted from taxable income. California places a limit of $100 per person annually of such deductions.

THE ELECTION OF JUDGES

Justices of the California Supreme Court and of the district courts of appeal are nominated and elected in the following manner. When the term of a sitting judge expires, the question is placed on the ballot: "Shall ———— be elected to office?" If a vacancy occurs or if the sitting judge does not wish to run for reelection, the governor nominates another person, whose nomination must be approved by a Commission of Qualification. His name is similarly placed on the ballot at the following election. If a majority of voters vote in the affirmative, the person thus nominated is elected. Otherwise the governor appoints some other person to fill the vacancy until the next election, when the above procedure is followed.

Judges of superior courts may be elected in the same manner, but no county has chosen to follow this procedure, and hence judges of lower courts are elected on a nonpartisan ballot as are other county officers. There is, however, a strong tradition for a sitting judge to be reelected, and vacancies which occur between elections are filled by the governor until the following election.

THE POLITICS OF NONPARTISANSHIP:
COUNTY, CITY, AND OTHER LOCAL ELECTIONS

Since 1913, county, city, and other local elections have been nonpartisan, that is, without party labels on the ballot. The absence of party labels, however, does not necessarily result in nonpartisan campaigns and elections. In Great Britain, where political parties are very strong, there are no party labels on the ballots for any election. California local elections, however, are for the most part truly nonpartisan. The national party organizations seldom openly sponsor candidates or otherwise participate in local elections but party leaders are often active and influential behind the scenes. The great majority of voters favor nonpartisanship in local elections and would not regard with favor candidates who run as partisans.

Party organizations and local political leaders, however, may exert an influence on local elections in more subtle and indirect ways without officially participating in local campaigns. They may avoid the front door and enter through the back. Acting as individuals and as civic groups, party leaders may sponsor candidates for local office and take an active part in campaigns, carefully avoiding any reference to their party ties. The extent to which party groups thus participate in local elections varies from one community to another. In some areas the impact of partisan politics on local elections is slight, but in others local elections are partisan in every respect but the form of the ballot.

Democratic clubs in some areas have openly participated in local campaigns, working for the election of Democratic candidates. Republican groups have generally been more astute, recognizing the public disapproval of partisanship in local elections, and have avoided identifying their candidates with party labels. The tie-in between national parties and local political groupings is often clearly revealed in national and state elections, when municipal and county officers put on other hats and become party officials and party candidates for office.

It would be a gross oversimplification, however, to conclude that nonpartisan elections are a sham and a humbug, the effect of which is to conceal partisan politics behind the façade of nonpartisanship. Nonpartisan elections do not end politics, and it would be unfortunate if they did. Politics, which is the art of governance, is needed in local governments as well as in the state and the nation. The politician plays an indispensable role in democratic society, and it is unfortunate that the term often is one of opprobrium. What should be recognized is that nonpartisan elections produce a different form of politics from that under partisan election.

Nonpartisan elections were adopted as a part of the municipal-reform movement which spread throughout the country in the early part of the present century. The rationale of nonpartisan elections is that there is no place in municipal, county, school, and other local elections for division of voters along national party lines; that there is no Democratic or Republican way to pave streets, to collect garbage, or to operate the local health department; that national party issues are not relevant to local governments. Local officials, it is said, should be elected solely on the basis of their qualifications for the duties of the office, and not because of their party affiliation. Party government at the local level was often marked by incompetence and corruption under the boss and machine system. Nonpartisan elections were adopted to enable the voters to elect honest and capable officials. "Keep politics out of our schools" was a slogan that was extended to other local affairs.

Generally speaking, the results have justified the claims that were made for nonpartisan elections. Municipal government, which formerly was termed a national disgrace, has been greatly reformed and its standards improved. Many cities are administered with a high degree of efficiency and economy, though the same cannot be said generally of county government.

Despite these improvements, nonpartisan elections have been criticized in recent years. It has come to be recognized that local governments not merely perform "housekeeping" functions, but also carry on important social services about which there may be important differences of policy. Most government programs today are being carried on jointly by the nation, the states, and the local units, and government policies are important at each level. The major criticism of nonpartisan elections, however, is that they have enabled the dominant element in many communities, usually the business group allied with the local newspaper, to control local governments and determine their policies, while other groups in the population, especially working classes, are unorganized and ineffective.[3] In some communities it is charged that the local government is a closed corporation run by a few business leaders or the courthouse gang.

Some Democrats have attacked nonpartisan elections as a device which enables Republican candidates, who usually have the support of the press, to be elected to a large majority of city and county offices even in strongly Democratic areas. A study committee of the CDC in 1959 urged the adoption of partisan elections in cities and counties, and a bill to this effect was passed by the Assembly Elections Committee in 1959 by a straight party vote, but died on the Assembly floor.

What are the actual effects of nonpartisan local elections? Are they nonpartisan in fact? Do they aid one party? Do they enable a small group to control local governments? Have they resulted in the election of better-qualified citizens to local office?

Fortunately a careful study of nonpartisan elections in California has been made by Professor Eugene Lee of the University of California, upon which the following summary is based.[4] This study indicates that Republicans hold a large majority of county, city, and other local offices, both elective and administrative. In 26 cities having more than 50,000 population each, 80 percent of the mayors and 69 percent of the city councilmen in 1955 were registered Republicans. In a majority of these cities the Democratic party had a majority of the registered voters, but in only four—Los Angeles, San Francisco, San Bernardino, and South Gate—were a majority of the councilmen Democrats. In six medium-sized cities in different parts of the state, whose elections were surveyed over a period of 25 years, the Republicans won 69 percent of the elections for mayor and councilmen, although in four of these cities the Democrats had a majority of the registered voters, and the other two were equally divided. Another significant finding is that a far larger percentage of Republican candi-

[3] Robert E. Lane, *Political Life* (Glencoe, Illinois: The Free Press, 1959), pp. 269–271.
[4] *The Politics of Nonpartisanship* (Berkeley: University of California Press, 1960).

dates than Democratic candidates won the elections. In these six cities, 45 percent of the Republican candidates won as compared with only 21 percent of the Democratic candidates.

Although these statistics indicate that Republican candidates won a substantial majority of local elective offices, even in communities where the Democrats led in the registration, the results were not necessarily due to the form of the ballot. About the same results obtained in state elections under a partisan ballot during the period. Other factors account in large part for the election of a majority of Republican candidates. A substantial majority of business and professional people—the group from which most local officers are drawn and probably would be drawn under any election system—are Republican. The local press, which greatly influences local elections, is Republican in most communities. It would appear also that Republican candidates are usually selected with greater care than are their opponents, receive more support, and more of them have had previous experience on advisory boards and in other civic activities.

The recruitment of candidates, a highly important aspect of politics, is conducted in different ways in the various communities. In many cities the city council itself acts as an informal recruiting body, appointing prospective candidates first to advisory bodies, and later selecting some to run for the city council when vacancies occur. In other cities an informal group of business and professional persons acts as a recruiting body, approaching citizens to run for office, and in a few cities an organized group performs this function. Almost everywhere it is recognized that the best-qualified citizens will seldom volunteer to run for public office unless they are urged to do so and are assured of support. Ordinarily the groups that recruit candidates for local office have difficulty in persuading leading citizens to run, and often have to approach many more persons than there are offices to be filled.

Most local election campaigns are conducted on the basis of the personal qualifications of the competing candidates. Issues play only a small part, but the same is true of most state contests.

The candidate with the largest personal acquaintance, who is favorably known in various organizations and civic groups, usually wins. The groups that are most influential in local election campaigns, in the order of their influence, are newspapers, merchants, service clubs, and women's organizations. Other groups have far less influence. Significantly, only one city in four reported that labor unions were influential in local elections, and political party organizations were influential in only one city in ten.

The attitude of various groups toward nonpartisan local elections is of significance. Of 46 editors who replied to a questionnaire, 40 favored nonpartisan elections and only four preferred partisan local elections. Approximately 90 percent of the mayors, city managers, and Republican county chairmen who replied favored nonpartisan local elections. Democratic county chairmen, however, favored partisan elections by about three to two.

There is little doubt but that public opinion generally favors nonpartisan local elections, and any attempt to return to partisan local elections will not succeed. If the Republican candidates have benefited by nonpartisan elections, it is because they have been chosen with greater care and have had greater public support than their opponents. Instead of seeking to repeal nonpartisan elections, Democratic groups should seek to arouse the interest of voters in local affairs, recruit well-qualified candidates for local offices, and give them support in the campaign, stressing, however, their qualifications rather than their partisanship.

chapter 4

Lawmakers and Lawmaking

☆

PRESSURE GROUPS

"Who Runs the State?" was the subject of an address by Governor Warren before the San Francisco Press Club shortly after the celebrated Lester Velie articles about Arthur Samish, "The Secret Boss of California," appeared in *Collier's* in August, 1949. One answer was given in a song for the occasion by Will Aubrey:

Who runs the state? You're going to get the answer.
Who runs the state? It's plain as can be.
Who runs the state? Is it really Arthur Samish?
No. It's the Southern Pacific and the P.G.&E.[1]

The Southern Pacific and the Pacific Gas and Electric Company do not run the state, although the Southern Pacific once did, and both are powerful on legislation which affects their interests. Other great corporations, including the Bank of America and the Standard Oil Company of California, are equally

---

[1] Quoted by Dean R. Cresap, *Party Politics in the Golden State* (Los Angeles: The Haynes Foundation, 1954) , p. 101.

influential. No longer are individual corporations the centers of power in state legislation and politics; today it is rather organized business, agricultural, labor, professional, and other groups. Because of the influence which these groups exert on legislative bodies, they are customarily known as interest or pressure groups. This does not necessarily mean, however, that they exert improper or unethical pressures on public officials. It is their business to follow the course of legislation affecting their membership, to keep their members advised, and to represent them before legislative committees and public bodies. These organizations are an essential aspect of a highly industrialized society. The information and advice which they offer on legislative problems are not only helpful to the legislator, but often constructive and in the public interest. There are organized pressure groups of many kinds: some are powerful while others are weak; some are ethical and others unethical; some are reformist and some are reactionary; some are active in politics while others abstain. Nowhere are pressure groups more highly organized and more potent than in California, for the state is big and has a highly diversified economy.

In the nonpartisan type of politics that has long prevailed in California, though it is now changing, organized interest or pressure groups play a highly influential role. Candidates face the necessity for raising large sums of money for election campaigns, for the cost of campaigning in California is high. Experienced legislators report that even an easy reelection may cost as much as $10,000. Although pressure groups do not directly contribute to election campaigns as a rule, their members do. The support or opposition of a powerful pressure group which has a large and influential membership, or which is able to raise substantial campaign contributions, is often a determining factor in election contests. Many organizations also have widespread public support outside their own membership. For these reasons pressure groups play a highly influential role in election campaigns and greatly influence the course of legislation.

More than 500 lobbyists representing well over 400 groups descend upon the state capital during legislative sessions, outnumbering legislators by more than four to one. The organizations they represent differ widely in strength and importance; some have large memberships; others speak for important sectors of the economy; many are weak, temporary, and relatively unimportant. The list of organizations with registered "legislative advocates" includes not only such powerful groups as the major oil companies, railroads, power companies, liquor and beer interests, motor carriers, major agricultural organizations, organized labor, and the potent teachers' lobby, but also the California Junior Statesmen of America, Citizens Committee for Home Rule, Women's Christian Temperance Union of Southern California, and the Committee to Save the Sea Lions.

Some of the most important of these organizations may be classified into the following groups, although the list is necessarily incomplete:

Agriculture—California Farm Bureau Federation, Grange, Associated Farmers, Agricultural Council, Farmers' Union, and many commodity organizations.
Labor—California Labor Federation AFL-CIO, Teamsters Legislative Council, the railway brotherhoods, and others.
Employers and business—California State Chamber of Commerce, Manufacturers Association, Taxpayers Association, and many individual business firms.
Other business interests—insurance, banking, retailers, grocers, real estate, hotels, building trades, fishing, canneries, and others, usually represented by trade associations.
Alcoholic-beverage industry—Malt Beverage Industry, major liquor, wine, and beer companies, and trade associations.
Public utilities—railways, gas and electric companies, motor bus and trucking industry.
Petroleum industry—major oil companies, independent smaller oil concerns.
Race tracks—Los Angeles and Hollywood turf clubs, other race tracks and industry associations.
Professional and other groups—American Medical Association,

Bar Association, dentists, osteopaths, plumbers, barbers, and many others.

Veterans' associations—American Legion, Veterans of Foreign Wars.

Public-welfare and old-age-assistance groups—California Institute of Social Welfare headed by George McLain, Old Age Pensioners, and others.

Local government—League of California Cities, County Supervisors Association, individual cities, counties, and other units of government.

Education—California Teachers' Association, Parent-Teacher Association, University of California, state colleges, other associations of school officers.

Public employees—State Employees' Association, Highway Patrolmen's Association, municipal and county employees, policemen, firemen, and others.

Reform organizations—League of Women Voters, Friends Committee on Legislation, Council of Churches, temperance societies, and others.

The lobbyists representing these and other organizations include some of the most astute and highly paid lawyers in the state, among them former speakers of the Assembly, former state senators and assemblymen, and other persons of prominence. Many are highly respected officials of trade associations and professional associations who have a wealth of expert information and are noted for accuracy. Others are relatively unknown and uninfluential.

Although the techniques used by these various organizations to influence legislation and public policy vary widely, most of them engage in some or all of the following activities: (1) representing their membership before legislative bodies, keeping in touch with pending measures, appearing before legislative committees, and keeping members advised concerning pending legislative bills; (2) initiating legislation in their interest and attempting to defeat legislative measures harmful to them; (3)

exerting influence and sometimes pressure on legislators; (4) issuing publicity in many forms to influence public opinion; (5) undertaking research, publishing a journal, organizing annual conferences, and performing other services for members. During election campaigns, pressure groups play quite different roles: some actively support their friends and oppose those whom they regard as unfriendly, while other groups refrain from openly participating in political campaigns. The sanction behind powerful pressure groups, however, is that they can deliver votes or campaign contributions or both to aid their friends and defeat their enemies.

The lobbying activities of organized pressure groups are usually open and aboveboard, with little of the venality formerly associated with the professional lobbyist. The legislative representatives at Sacramento, as a rule, command the respect and attention of members of the legislature because of their standing, reliability, and expertness. Few today conform to the stereotype of the corrupt lobbyist who influenced legislators by bribes, entertainment, or blackmail. It is not only legitimate but highly desirable for each branch of business, industry, agriculture, labor, and other walks of life to be represented before the legislature. The lobby or "Third House," as it is often called, was given a black eye in the state by the exposure of the unethical methods and power of Arthur Samish, formerly known as "Mr. Big" among the lobbyists until convicted in 1953 for evasion of federal income taxes. A series of sensational articles exposing his operations appeared in *Collier's* in 1949. Ten years earlier the same facts had been brought out in the report of the Philbrick legislative investigating committee. Samish was known to represent the liquor and beer interests, and at times represented railroads, trucking, bus lines, and race tracks, although he never let it be known precisely who were his clients. His power was based on the large funds at his disposal to contribute to the campaigns of friendly legislators and to oppose those who did not go along with him, plus a large staff which kept him informed on legislative developments.

Following the exposure of Samish in 1949, a special session of the legislature which was called by Governor Warren enacted a law regulating lobbying. Under it anyone who is engaged to attempt to influence legislation must register as a legislative advocate and regularly file reports indicating by whom he is employed and for what purpose, the legislation with which he is concerned, the compensation received, and monthly expenses. Governor Warren proposed a much more stringent bill which required in addition reports from firms and associations who employed lobbyists, and their campaign contributions, but this was not accepted by the legislature.

The law regulating legislative advocates has brought their activities out in the open and has given legislators greater independence of their influence. No longer are lobbyists seen on the floor of the legislature directing the legislative fights. With new and handsome quarters for the legislature, better salaries for legislators, and better staff, it has acquired far greater dignity and self-respect. The "Third House" still retains its power and influence, but operates more openly and serves an indispensable function in the legislative process. The legislature of today has greatly improved standing and prestige in comparison with that of several decades ago. It is a far cry from the famous first legislature, known as the "legislature of 1,000 drinks."

THE PRESS

From its earliest days, the California press played an active role in the political life of the state, often dominating political parties and exerting considerable influence in election campaigns. The California press was and still is overwhelmingly Republican. In the 1960 presidential campaign, 65 newspapers with a total circulation of 3,797,660 favored Nixon, 20 newspapers with a circulation of 471,871 favored Kennedy, and 10 independents had a circulation of 172,986.[2] In 1964, however, many Republican newspapers gave Goldwater only lukewarm support and some supported Johnson. In the absence of strong party organizations,

---

[2] *Editor and Publisher*, November 5, 1960.

the press exerts a strong influence in public affairs; all political candidates seek newspaper support and in local elections few can be elected without it.

The impact of the press on political affairs, however, has been undergoing change. Rising costs of newspaper production coupled with the population explosion in metropolitan areas have forced the press to become preoccupied with the competitive race of building new circulation and of appealing to a large and more diversified audience. The once vigorous, often strident, political voice of the press has softened and there is a trend toward political "nonpartisanship" or "mild partisanship." The large Democratic registration majority may well be a factor. With the elimination of cross filing, the resurgent political organizations, radio, and television have created alternative channels of communication in partisan elections.

California, like the rest of the nation, has witnessed the merger of city daily newspapers until today only a single newspaper, or a single publisher, is found in most cities. Only in Los Angeles, San Francisco, Oakland, and Sacramento are there competing publishers—all Republican with the exception of the *Sacramento Bee*. It is significant that in the four largest metropolitan areas of Los Angeles, San Francisco, Oakland, and San Diego, there is no Democratic daily newspaper. This was a major reason why the Democrats, with a registration of nearly a million more voters than the Republicans, were unable from 1942 until 1958 to carry state elections.

Although the press, with a few notable exceptions, is predominantly Republican, it has increasingly reported the news in a nonpartisan manner, and has confined its partisanship largely to the editorial page. After the 1962 election, Richard M. Nixon, Republican candidate for governor, complained bitterly about the press coverage of the campaign, whereas Edmund G. Brown, the Democratic candidate, praised the press for fair and objective reporting of the campaign. What Nixon objected to was that press accounts of his speeches contained not only what he said, but background information. Doubtless the background information deflated some of his charges against the Brown administration.

Incumbents in office, regardless of party, have an important advantage over their political opponents because they are able to make the news throughout the years and to secure press, radio, and television coverage. The Democratic party has been able to capitalize on this advantage because a large majority of federal and state officials are Democrats.

Apart from the problem of a one-party press, another and perhaps more significant problem exists today. Many nonmetropolitan newspapers, despite their "hometown" orientation, are papers of "consensus," avoiding controversial local issues; some are indifferent to local problems and still others are "merchant dominated," representing the point of view of the community's power structure. In view of the acute problems of urban growth in California, there is a danger that newspapers will fail to create an informed public opinion, which is necessary to meet these problems.

In national elections the radio and television compete with the press as media for reaching the voters, but they are not equally adapted for use in state and local elections. The cost is extremely high, and state and local candidates are usually unable to compete effectively with the counterattractions provided by commercially supported programs. Candidates for Congress or the state Assembly cannot afford to hire a metropolitan television station that blankets the entire area. The more promising future role of radio and television in the area of public affairs is through panel discussions, documentaries, and editorials dealing with important national, state, and local issues. Educational television offers numerous public-affairs programs, and commercial television is also entering the field. Radio, especially FM, increasingly dependent upon special audiences, may provide the "many voices" necessary in a democratic society.

THE POLITICS OF THE LEGISLATURE

In his first inaugural address in 1911 Hiram Johnson said, "There can be no partisan approach to state lawmaking." Nonpartisanship was the usual rule not only during the period that

California was a one-party state, when the Democrats elected only a handful of legislators and obviously party division would be meaningless, but continued until the 1950s. Joseph Beek, Secretary of the State Senate, wrote in 1942 that in each house of the legislature there was a different alignment upon almost every issue, but there were few votes in which the parties divided.[3] Even today, with the resurgence of partisanship, there are relatively few bills on which there is a clear-cut division between the two parties. The vast majority of the two thousand-odd measures passed by each biennial-long session of the legislature are non-controversial. Many are technical revisions of the statutes. The large majority of bills are passed without opposition. On many important subjects, such as highways, education, health, and state institutions, there is no party division.

In recent sessions of the legislature, however, party voting has been more frequent. Governor Brown was able in 1959 to secure the passage of a sweeping legislative program by a party vote. Today there are a score or more key bills at each session upon which there is a party vote in one or both houses. Both major political parties in the Assembly now hold weekly caucuses at which the most important measures are discussed, and often a consensus is reached, though no attempt is made to bind members. The Senate does not have similar party caucuses, but members often attend the party caucuses of the Assembly. Seniority and the personal standing of members are extremely important in the leadership of the Senate, while in the Assembly the speaker, the party floor leaders and whips, and the chairmen of the most important committees provide the leadership.

The politics of the legislature reflects the pluralism of society in the state, and the different sectional, economic, and other groupings, rather than party lines. On some issues there may be a north-south division, as in the protracted water fight; on other issues the division may be between urban and rural members, though this is rare; and on still others the division may reflect

---

[3] *The California Legislature* (Sacramento: State Printing Office, 1950 edition), p. 149.

prolabor or promanagement attitudes. The number and variety of such divisions are great, reflecting the various interests that are dominant in different parts of the state. As James Madison wrote in *The Federalist* papers, the regulation of these various and conflicting interests is the principal task of legislation.

The election of the speaker of the Assembly is the most important contest in the organization of the legislature. The speaker appoints the standing committees, a fact of utmost importance to members, and selects the committee chairmen. The composition of the major standing committees greatly influences legislative action. Formerly certain lobbyists and pressure groups played a key role in the selection of the speaker and were influential in the selection of the members of the committees which passed upon legislation of interest to them. Fortunately this practice has largely disappeared. The election of James W. Silliman as speaker in 1953 and the following election of Luther H. (Abe) Lincoln in 1955 and 1957 marked the overthrow of lobby domination of the election of the speaker. The fights over the speakership in the past have usually turned upon coalitions of members of both parties. Members on the winning side expected and secured good committee assignments.

Contrary to the practice in Congress, members of both political parties are appointed as chairmen of standing committees, though the chairmanships of major committees are usually held by members of the majority party. Seniority is given great weight in the selection of committee chairmen in the Senate, but junior members are often appointed as committee chairmen in the Assembly.

Since 1958 there has been a marked increase in the partisanship of the legislature, especially the Assembly, in passing on the governor's bills and his budget. Democratic members have generally supported the governor's program for increased government activities in public health, welfare, education, state institutions, parks and recreation, and in other fields, while the Republicans have usually opposed increased expenditures and new taxes. Acting as an economy bloc, the Republican members of the Assem-

California Congressional Districts, 1961

bly have frequently held up the passage of the governor's budget, which requires a two-thirds majority, demanding that a number of cuts be made. Although the reductions have been small in relation to the total budget, they are used as a means of attacking the increasing cost of government under the Democratic administration. And Governor Brown has faced not only Republican opposition to his program, but also increasing difficulty in securing the support of the members of his own party in the Assembly, who take their cue from Speaker Jesse Unruh.

The politics of the state Senate is quite different from that of the Assembly; it is much less partisan and more influenced by senior members who have risen to positions of leadership. It is often said in Sacramento that the Assembly is a group but the Senate is a club.

LEGISLATIVE APPORTIONMENT

On October 27, 1965, Governor Brown signed into law an act redistricting the state for the election of both houses of the legislature on the basis of population, thus ending a controversy which had lasted for more than thirty years. The reapportionment of the Senate by population was strongly opposed by the Senate, whose members sought in various ways to avoid compliance with the *Reynolds v. Sims* decision of the United States Supreme Court in 1964, which had held that both houses of the state legislatures must be apportioned on the basis of population. Speaking for the Court, Chief Justice Warren had stated:

Legislators represent people, not trees or acres. Legislators are elected by voters, not farms or cities or economic interests. . . . Weighting the votes of citizens differently, by any method or means, merely because of where they happen to reside, hardly seems justifiable. . . . Full and effective participation by all citizens in state government requires, therefore, that each citizen have an equally effective voice in the election of members of his state legislature. Modern and viable state government needs, and the Constitution demands, no less. . . . A citizen, a qualified voter, is no more nor no less so because he lives in the city or on the farm. . . . This is the clear and strong command of our Consti-

tution's Equal Protection Clause . . . [which] demands no less than substantially equal state legislative representation for all citizens, of all
places as well as all races.[4]

Relying on this decision, a United States District Court held
that the apportionment of the state Senate was unconstitutional
in 1964, but deferred any judicial action until after July 1, 1965,
in order to give the legislature an opportunity to reapportion
the Senate so as to meet the requirements of the federal Constitution.

Reapportionment was the first order of business when the
California legislature met in January, 1965, but the Assembly
and the Senate were unable to agree and adjourned without
action. The legislature, however, passed a resolution memorial-
izing Congress to submit a constitutional amendment to the
states to permit apportionment of one house of a state legislature
on a basis other than population, if approved by the voters of the
state, and voted funds to send a delegation to visit other state
legislatures to urge them to support such an amendment. The
failure of the Dirksen constitutional amendment in 1965 to secure the required two-thirds vote in the United States Senate
crushed any hope of securing an amendment to the United States
Constitution in time to avoid reapportionment of the California
Senate.

After the legislature adjourned in 1965 without reapportion-
ing the Senate in compliance with the ruling of the United States
Supreme Court, a citizen petition was filed with the California
Supreme Court seeking a writ of mandate to require reapportionment of the Senate. The Court accepted jurisdiction and on
September 1, 1965, handed down a decision requiring the legislature to reapportion both houses by not later than December 9,
1965. Reapportionment by this date was necessary if it was to
become effective in the primary and general elections in 1966.
Although the Assembly had supposedly been apportioned on the

---

[4] *Reynolds v. Sims*, 377 U.S. 533, 562, 563, 565, 568.

California State Assembly Districts, 1965

California State Senatorial Districts, 1965

basis of population in 1961, the Court held that the differences in population of the districts were in some instances so great as to deny equal protection required by the federal Constitution. The largest district had a population of 306,191 in 1960, and that of the smallest was 72,105.

The California Supreme Court laid down two guidelines for reapportionment according to population: no district should vary by more than 15 percent from the average population of all districts (the rule adopted by the House of Representatives in a bill pending in Congress); and second, a majority of the members of each house should be elected by voters of districts containing at least 48 percent of the population of the state. Finally, the Court announced that if the legislature failed to reapportion both houses by December 9, it would order a temporary redistricting of the state to be effective in the 1966 elections, and released the details of the Court's reapportionment plan.

The legislature could no longer delay reapportionment; if it failed to act the Supreme Court would put its own plan into effect. Meeting at the call of the governor in October, 1965, it moved promptly to reapportion both houses on the basis of population. Only a few changes were required in the boundaries of the Assembly districts, but a complete revision of the Senate districts was necessary. As required by the California Supreme Court, the Senate apportionment of 1965 achieved substantial equality in the population of districts. The least populous district had 337,629 residents, while the most populous district had 441,482 (1960 Census statistics). This spread was in great contrast to that of the 1961 apportionment, in which one mountain district had a population of 14,196, and the most populous district, Los Angeles County, had over 6 million. The ten least populous senatorial districts in the 1961 apportionment, which together had 3.3 percent of the state population, received 25 percent of the Senate seats, the same number allocated to the ten most populous counties, which had 69.5 percent of the population of the state.

The Senate apportionment prior to 1965 was criticized on

the ground that the rural counties were overrepresented on the basis of population and the larger metropolitan counties under-represented, and that the 50 northern counties were overrepre-sented and the 8 counties south of the Tehachapi Mountains were underrepresented. Table III shows that the southern coun-ties and metropolitan counties throughout the state received representation in proportion to their population in the 1965 apportionment. The number of seats allocated to the northern counties, which had 43 percent of the population of the state in 1960, was reduced from 32 to 18, and the number allocated to the 8 southern counties, which had 57 percent of the state popula-tion, was increased from 8 to 22. Even more striking was the reduction of the seats allocated to the 41 nonmetropolitan coun-ties from 23 to 6, and the corresponding increase of the seats allocated to metropolitan counties from 17 to 34. The rule of

TABLE III. COMPARISON OF THE 1961 AND 1965 SENATE APPORTIONMENTS [a]

	Percent of state population	Number of Senate seats			
		1961		1965	
		No.	Percent	No.	Percent
50 northern counties	43	32	80	18	45
8 southern counties	57	8	20	22	55
17 metropolitan counties [b]	86.4	17	42.5	34 [c]	85
41 nonmetropolitan counties	13.6	23	57.5	6	15

[a] Statistics on population and apportionment are taken from Don A. Allen, Sr., *Legislative Sourcebook*, published by the California Assembly (Sac-ramento: State Printing Office, 1965).

[b] Metropolitan counties are those included within "standard metropoli-tan statistical areas" as defined by the United States Bureau of the Census.

[c] Allowance is made for 4 nonmetropolitan counties (with a combined population sufficient to form one senatorial district), which were merged with metropolitan counties to form senatorial districts.

"one man—one vote" was put into effect by the 1965 apportionment. Los Angeles County, which formerly held only one seat, was allocated 14 and shared another with a part of adjoining Orange County; San Diego and Alameda each received 2 seats and shared a third; San Francisco, 2; Orange, Santa Clara, and Sacramento, 1 each and shared another; and 5 metropolitan counties—Marin, Solano, San Joaquin, Kern, and Santa Barbara —which did not have sufficient population to form a district, were combined with an adjoining county.

The Senate elected in 1966 from all 40 senatorial districts necessarily lost many of its former members from the rural, mountain, and less populous counties, many of whom had served long periods. Their places were taken by new members from Los Angeles and the other large metropolitan counties. Control passed from the northern counties to the south, from the less populous counties to the large metropolitan counties. Only 26 of the 37 incumbent senators (3 seats were vacant) entered the 1966 primaries; 22 were nominated and 4 were defeated, three by other incumbents. In the general election 18 incumbents were reelected, including 3 Republicans who defeated Democratic incumbents. Twenty members of the Assembly ran for the Senate in the 1966 primaries, and 17 were nominated. The Senate in 1967, accordingly, has almost as many former members of the Assembly as former Senators, and the large majority of its members are experienced legislators.

How will these changes in the membership of the Senate affect its work and its role in state politics? Before attempting to discuss the probable effects of apportionment of the Senate according to population, let us review the national background of the controversy over legislative apportionment, a background that long antedates California's admission to the Union.

In the early history of the country the vast majority of the people lived on farms and in small towns, and there was little or no controversy over the representation of rural and urban populations in the state legislatures. In 1790 only 5 percent of the population lived in cities; fifty years later the urban population had increased to only 10.8 percent. Following the Civil War, the growing industrialization was accompanied by the rapid growth of cities. By 1900 urban population had risen to 40 percent and it passed the 50-percent mark by 1920. In the 1960s approximately two-thirds of the population reside in metropolitan areas as defined by the Census Bureau. California has become one of the most urbanized states.

Until around 1900 population was the usual basis of representation in both houses of the state legislatures. The original constitutions of 36 of the 50 states provided for the apportionment of both houses of the legislature on the basis of population. The Northwest Ordinance, which was enacted by Congress in 1787, the year the Constitution was adopted, provided for "proportionate representation of the people in the legislatures" established in the territories. The original constitutions of all of the states admitted to the Union before 1883, including California, provided that both houses of the legislature be apportioned on the basis of population.

After the rapid increase in urban population during the latter part of the nineteenth century, however, many legislatures failed to comply with the state constitutional requirement that the legislature be apportioned according to population. State legislatures dominated by rural counties refused to allocate additional seats to the rapidly growing urban areas, which would have necessitated reducing the number of seats for rural areas. In some states, as in Illinois and Tennessee, the legislature refused for more than fifty years to reapportion the state, despite great shifts in population. Because of the deadlock over reapportionment and the refusal of rural legislators to give up seats to the rapidly growing urban counties, many states repealed or modified the constitutional requirement that the state legislature be apportioned according to population. Apportionment by counties or other local governmental units, sometimes in combination with population, was widely adopted for one or both houses. In 1926, California amended its constitution to provide that the Assembly be apportioned according to population and the Senate by counties. In fourteen states the constitution itself apportioned one or both houses, allocating the seats by named governmental units. Georgia and Maryland not only apportioned legislative seats so as to insure rural domination of the state legislature, but also adopted the "county unit" system for the election of executive officers and members of Congress. All of these various methods of apportionment had the same purpose, namely, to give greater representation to voters in rural and less populous areas than to voters in urban areas. By 1960 the constitutions of only seven states required apportionment of both houses on the basis of population.

In 1964, when the United States Supreme Court ruled that both houses of the state legislatures must be apportioned on the basis of population, more than forty states failed to meet this requirement in one or both houses. A study published in 1961 comparing the value or weight of votes cast for members of the legislature in rural and urban counties throughout the country indicated that the value of a vote cast in counties with less than 25,000 population was 171 (100 being the average vote value), while a vote cast in counties of 500,000 population and over had a value of only 76, and in counties between 100,000 and 500,000 population, only 81.[5] In other words, votes cast in rural counties had an average value more than twice as great as votes cast in urban counties. The number of urban voters required to elect a representative in the legislature was twice as great as the number of rural voters. Moreover, the devaluation of urban and suburban votes was rapidly increasing. In 1910 the value of votes cast in counties with less than 25,000 population was 113; by 1960 it had increased to 171, while the value of votes cast in urban counties had declined. The greatest devaluation of votes has occurred not in the core cities, most of which have declined in population in recent decades, but rather in the burgeoning suburbs of large cities.

---

[5] Paul A. David and Ralph Eisenberg, *Devaluation of Urban and Suburban Votes* (Charlottesville: Bureau of Public Administration, University of Virginia, 1961), p. 9.

The controversy over legislative apportionment did not become acute in California until after 1920. The legislature had previously redistricted the state after each decennial census on the basis of population, as required by the state constitution, although it deadlocked in the 1911 session and had to be called back in special session to enact the reapportionment. After the 1920 census, however, the legislature failed to redistrict the state; doing so would have required the 50 northern counties to give up 4 seats in the Senate and 8 in the Assembly to the 8 counties south of the Tehachapis. The southern counties had approximately 40 percent of the state population in 1920, but only 30 percent of the seats in the legislature under the 1911 apportionment.[6] It was evident that by 1930 they would have a majority of the residents of the state. Los Angeles County was growing at a phenomenal rate and by 1930 had 39 percent of the population of the state. The northern counties foresaw their own subordination and refused to reapportion the state legislature as required by the Constitution. Holding 70 percent of the seats under the 1911 reapportionment, they were easily able to block reapportionment.

In 1926, after the legislature had failed during three regular biennial sessions to reapportion the state, a Los Angeles group placed an initiative on the ballot to force the reapportionment of the state on the basis of population as provided in the state constitution. Faced with the threatened loss of rural seats in both houses of the legislature, the leading agricultural associations (with the active support not only of the rural counties, but also the chambers of commerce and other business, industrial, and civic organizations of the large cities) countered with an alternative reapportionment plan that was presented to the voters as a compromise between the rural and urban counties. This proposal, which was called the "federal plan," retained the apportionment of the Assembly on the basis of population and provided

---

[6] Statistics on population and apportionment are taken from Don A. Allen, Sr., *Legislative Sourcebook,* published by the California Assembly (Sacramento: State Printing Office, 1965).

that the Senate would be apportioned by counties or areas. Since it was not possible to allocate a senator to each of the 58 counties without increasing the size of the Senate, it provided that not more than three counties could be combined in a senatorial district, but no county could be allocated more than one senator.

Proponents of the "federal plan" contended that the plan of representation that had proved successful in Congress should be followed in the state legislature, and would assure representation of the rural areas and agricultural interests which were very important to the state. Contending that the urban voters would determine the election of the governor and other statewide executive officers, and elect a majority of the members of the Assembly and of Congress, they maintained that it was only reasonable and fair to permit the rural counties to retain control of the state Senate, without which they would have no effective voice in state government. The proposal for reapportionment of both houses according to population lost, and the "federal plan" carried by a substantial majority. Two years later, before it went into effect, it was challenged at the polls by a referendum and was approved by the voters by an increased majority.

In 1948 the AFL-CIO sponsored an initiative to reapportion the Senate on the basis of population, but limited any county to 10 members. The proposal would have increased the number of senators allocated to Los Angeles and other large metropolitan counties, and decreased those assigned to the rural and mountain counties. Organized labor evidently believed that a different basis of apportionment was necessary in order to elect a Senate that would be more liberal in outlook and sympathetic to the problems of the great cities and labor. The arguments advanced in favor of the amendment, however, did not stress the conservatism of the Senate but rather the principle that every voter ought to have an equal voice in electing legislative representatives.

The initiative was strongly opposed not only by the rural counties that would have lost seats but also by the chambers of commerce and other business and civic groups in the urban counties that would have gained seats. Opponents labeled the initiative a dangerous, radical measure that would turn over control of the state government to the labor unions and political bosses of the large cities. The measure was defeated by an overwhelming majority, failing to carry a single county, even Los Angeles County which would have received 10 Senate seats instead of 1.

The urban population of the state continued to increase at a rapid rate, while the nonurban population remained relatively stable, making the Senate membership increasingly unrepresentative of the population of the state. In 1960 the ten metropolitan areas of the state had 86.4 percent of the state population, but held only 17 Senate seats (42.5 percent), while the nonmetropolitan counties with 13.6 percent of the population held 23 seats (57.5 percent). The 4 percent of the state population residing in the 21 northernmost counties elected 10 members of the Senate while the 57 percent of the population residing in the 8 southern counties elected only 8.

In 1960 an initiative to increase the number of senators assigned to the large urban counties, with a limit that no county could receive more than 7, was submitted by a group in the southern part of the state, headed by Frank G. Bonelli, Chairman of the Los Angeles County Board of Supervisors. It was defeated by a two-to-one vote, carrying only Los Angeles County.

In 1961, on the recommendation of the governor, the legislature created a commission of leading citizens to make a thorough study of the subject of legislative representation. After conducting hearings throughout the state, the commission recommended in 1962 that any county having more than 1,500,000 population should have one additional senator for each 1,500,000 or fraction thereof above that number, but that no county should have more than four senators. Under this proposal Los Angeles County would have gained three additional senators, but other metropolitan counties would not have qualified for an additional seat. No other change in the existing apportionment was recommended. The rural counties would not have lost any seats, but when additional seats were required the number of members of the

Senate would have been increased. The commission defended its recommendation to give Los Angeles County three additional senators on the ground that one senator could not adequately represent the varied interests of 6 million people.

The plan received no support in the Senate. Speaker Jesse Unruh, a member of the commission, introduced a bill in the Assembly to submit the plan to the voters; but as an inducement that might secure the two-thirds majority required for a proposed constitutional amendment, amended the plan to provide that five other metropolitan counties would each receive an additional senator. This bill was killed in committee in the Senate, and a counterproposal to create another study commission was rejected by the Assembly on the ground that action rather than a study commission was needed.

After the legislature failed to act on the recommendation of the 1961 ribbon commission, a group of business and civic leaders and public officials in southern California, led by Supervisor Bonelli of Los Angeles County, sponsored a similar initiative—Proposition No. 23—which would have increased the size of the Senate to fifty members and allocated the additional seats to the six largest metropolitan counties (five to Los Angeles County and one each to San Francisco, Alameda, San Diego, Orange, and Santa Clara Counties). The initiative was supported by civic and business organizations in Los Angeles and San Diego Counties, but elsewhere in the state was opposed not only by farm organizations and the rural counties but also by chambers of commerce and various business and civic groups in the large cities. According to reports filed with the secretary of state, three-fourths of the funds opposing the measure were contributed by sixteen large corporations, including a large public utility, several leading oil companies, large banks, railroads, and one New York public-relations firm. The Association of County Supervisors, the California League of Cities, and 57 county boards of supervisors (all except Los Angeles County) passed resolutions in opposition. The press, except in Los Angeles and San Diego Counties, generally opposed the measure. The AFL-CIO, which had sponsored the 1948 initiative to apportion the Senate on the basis of population, came out in opposition.

Proposition 23 carried Los Angeles and Orange Counties by nearly a million majority; but since this was not enough to overcome the large majorities against it in the other 56 counties, it lost by a vote of 2,181,758 for and 2,495,440 against. In Los Angeles County the vote was three to one in favor, but in the 50 northern counties the measure lost by the same ratio. Four of the six counties which would have received additional seats in the Senate rolled up large majorities against the measure.

Five times the voters of the state rejected proposals to give larger representation in the Senate to Los Angeles County and other large metropolitan counties. The opposition of the rural counties and farm organizations to any change in the apportionment of the Senate is understandable, but the opposition from the chambers of commerce, large corporations, leading banks, and various business and civic groups in the large cities, and from the large majority of voters of urban counties requires some explanation.

The controversy over the apportionment of the Senate was not, in fact, a struggle for power between the rural and urban counties, as is often supposed. Nor was it primarily a struggle between the North and the South, though the northern counties, rural and urban, feared the dominance of the Senate by Los Angeles County, which they believed would result if the Senate was apportioned according to population. The other southern counties also feared the dominance of Los Angeles County and voted against the several proposals to give it more seats in the Senate. The struggle was primarily a contest between conservatives and liberals. Conservatives wanted a Senate that would act as a restraint on liberal legislation passed by the Assembly, a majority of whose members were elected by the large cities. From 1931 to 1956 the Senate was strongly conservative, which attitude conservative groups attributed largely to the "federal plan" of apportionment. Business groups in the large cities opposed apportionment of the Senate according to population, which they believed would result in the election of a more liberal body. On the other hand, liberals favored apportionment by population because they desired a more liberal Senate. The Senators elected from sparsely settled counties were, as a rule, attorneys or businessmen whose outlooks on most public issues were similar to those held by businessmen, bankers, and industrialists in the large cities. As one acute observer has pointed out, for many years the Senate was ruled by a powerful clique of men who had long served in the legislature.

Many had great wealth and commanded great respect in their own counties. They were vigorous minded, politically adroit, genuinely interested in government, and they relished their power and their prowess. . . . They came from such places as Newman, El Centro, Marysville, Angels Camp, and San Bernardino.[7]

This ruling group retired and the strongly conservative Senate came to an end in the 1950s. By 1959 the Democrats had a better than two-to-one majority in the Senate, stronger than their majority in the Assembly. The Senate was no longer a bastion of conservatism, though it was still ruled by a small group of senior members.

Only time will reveal the effects of apportionment of the Senate on the basis of population. The change has increased the representation, hence the power, of the metropolitan counties, especially Los Angeles County, and reduced that of the northern rural counties. It has likewise shifted representation and power from the north to the south, where a majority of the people reside. Whether the senators elected from the metropolitan counties, or those elected from the south, will vote as a bloc remains to be seen. Before reapportionment, members of the Senate rarely voted as a regional bloc, nor was there a north-south division except when there was a definite regional issue, as the transportation of water from the north to the south. Even when there was

---

[7] Mary Ellen Leary, "The Legislature" in *California State Government: Its Tasks and Organization* (New York: American Assembly, Columbia University, 1956) , p. 22.

a definite regional issue, which was uncommon, it was usually resolved by a compromise. As a rule, conservatives from all parts of the state have voted together on controversial social and economic issues, and liberals have done the same. On the great majority of issues before the legislature, however, there is no conservative or liberal position, but like-minded members on each particular issue have joined together. It is unlikely that the change in the apportionment of the Senate will alter this practice.

Since the Senate will in all probability continue to be a more conservative body than the Assembly, the fears of conservatives may prove to be unfounded. Because of its greater prestige, power, and the opportunity which it affords its members to render distinguished public service, the Senate will continue to attract persons of greater maturity, experience, and standing in their own communities than those attracted to the Assembly. Conservatism in the late 1960s is strongest in the three large metropolitan counties in the south, which received fifteen additional members of the Senate—Los Angeles, Orange, and San Diego. It is likely that a majority of the new senators from these counties will be conservative in outlook, regardless of party label. Despite the fact that the senatorial districts have been gerrymandered in favor of the Democratic party, the Republicans will in all probability gain strength in the new Senate. If the Republicans capture control of the legislature in 1971 and are able to reapportion the state, they stand to make substantial gains in the membership of both houses from these three counties.

Will the agricultural and rural interests of the state be adequately represented in the new Senate? Although the rural counties have lost roughly three-fourths of their seats in the Senate, it should be noted that seven of the metropolitan counties, including Los Angeles, are also leading agricultural counties. It is quite unlikely that the new Senate will ride roughshod over the rural and agricultural interests of the state. Probably smaller portions of state highway funds will be spent in the future in the rural counties of the north and more in the urban counties, especially in the south, but few if any other changes in state policies that can be attributed to the changed membership of the Senate are likely to occur.

Because of the shift from the north to the south, of population, political power, and a majority of the members of the Senate, it has been urged that the state be divided into two states—North and South. This proposal should not be taken seriously. The two sections of the state are interdependent and are united by many ties—historical, economic, political, cultural, and other. Dissolution, even were it possible (which it is not), would greatly harm both sections and destroy the greatness of California. For eighty years the northern part of the state had a large majority of the population and dominated both houses of the state legislature. During this period legislative members from the north and the south worked together cooperatively and harmoniously, and there is no reason to assume that they will not do so in the future.

The representation controversy has presumably been resolved in favor of apportionment of the Senate on the basis of population, but the problem of political gerrymandering of the state—to the advantage of the party in power and to accommodate the desires and ambitions of individual members of the legislature—continues unabated. The political gerrymanders by the Republicans in 1951 and the Democrats in 1961 were both skillfully made to achieve the maximum advantage to the party in office by giving it a disproportionate share of the legislative representatives. The greatest opportunity for the political gerrymander occurs in large cities with multiple districts, which can be carved in grotesque shapes to achieve the desired results.

Almost any district in Los Angeles County could be used as an example of a gerrymander. The two districts shown on the accompanying page are not atypical. Districts of unusual shapes are indicative, but not necessarily proof, of a gerrymander. A knowledge of the voting habits of the voters of the area is essential to understand the nature and extent of the gerrymander. Assembly District No. 54 is an example of a "shoestring"

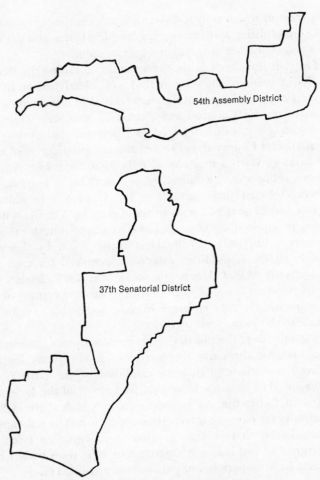

Two Legislative Districts in Los Angeles County

district, extending from Monrovia and Arcadia on the east, skirting south of Pasadena, to Glendale on the west. It is difficult to conceive of reasons other than partisan for the formation of a district from such widely separated municipalities and parts of municipalities. Senate District No. 37, which extends from Long

Legislative Apportionment · 111

Beach (part of which is included), with frequent jogs and turns, to take in Whittier and intervening municipalities and agricultural areas, is another example of a gerrymander.

The political effects of the gerrymander following the Democratic redistricting of the state in 1961 were clearly shown in the 1962 election. The Democratic party received 51.8 percent of the two-party vote for Congress and elected 25 members, while the Republican party, which received 48.2 percent, elected only 13. In Los Angeles County the effects of the gerrymander were even more striking. With a majority of only 7,726 votes out of more than two million cast, a difference of less than ½ percent, the Democrats elected their candidates for 11 of the 15 seats in Congress and 23 of the 31 seats in the Assembly.[8] For the state as a whole, it required 207,000 votes to elect a Republican member of Congress, but only 115,000 Democratic votes. In the state Assembly 90,000 Republican votes were required for each seat won, but only 58,000 Democratic votes. The 1970 election will see a tremendous drive by both parties to capture control of the legislature and elect the governor in order to be able to redistrict the state to the victor's advantage.

Not only does the political gerrymander distort the election results to favor the party in power, but it also lends itself to stacking the districts so that the candidate of one party is virtually assured of election. More than 80 percent of the legislative districts in California are safe districts in which there is little opportunity for effective interparty competition. The only apparent solution is to take the function of redistricting from the legislature and vest it in a nonpartisan or bipartisan body whose members have no personal or partisan interest to serve.

THE INITIATIVE AND REFERENDUM

Although the initiative and referendum are widely used throughout the country, in no other state are they used as extensively as

---

[8] The election statistics have been taken from Totton J. Anderson and Eugene C. Lee, "The 1962 Election in California," 16 *Western Political Quarterly* 396–420 (1963), at p. 417.

in California.[9] It is not unusual for as many as 20 state propositions and a number of local measures to be submitted to the
voters at a single election. Many of these are technical and
involved; often they are highly controversial. Despite some exceptions, voters of the state have usually exercised the power of
direct legislation wisely and with discrimination. This is a continuing source of amazement to students of politics, particularly
to visitors from other states.

From 1938 until 1956 initiative proposals for liberal old-age
pensions and other expensive forms of welfare provisions were
placed on the ballot at almost every election. Except in 1948, these
measures were regularly voted down by the voters, and the plan
adopted in 1948 was repealed by the voters two years later. Various proposals have been made for constitutional amendments to
restrict the use of the initiative in order to avoid the necessity of
voting on such measures at almost every election, but the voters
of the state appear to be well satisfied with the initiative, and so
far have been unwilling to approve any restriction of its use.

The initiative and referendum were adopted in 1911, during
the Progressive reform movement which swept the country and
resulted in their adoption in many other states. The earlier
domination of the state legislature by political bosses and the
Southern Pacific Railroad had discredited it in the minds of the
voters and led to the revision of the constitution to permit these
forms of direct legislation by the voters. Through the initiative a
group of voters may submit proposed legislation or constitutional
amendments to the voters, while the referendum is used to provide for a popular vote on laws enacted by the state legislature.

To put an initiative proposal on the ballot, either to amend
the state constitution or to enact new legislation, a petition

---

[9] The author has made extensive use in the following account of the excellent study of Winston W. Crouch, *The Initiative and Referendum in California* (Los Angeles: The Haynes Foundation, 1950). See also California Assembly Interim Committee on Constitutional Amendments, "Background Study
on the Initiative," November, 1965 (mimeograph).

containing the signatures equal to 8 percent of the number of qualified voters who voted for governor at the preceding general election is required. No distinction is made in the numbers of signatures required to submit a constitutional amendment and to submit a simple legislative enactment. As a result, most initiative proposals have been in the form of constitutional amendments, and California has thus written much legislation into the state constitution.

An initiative petition must be submitted 130 days prior to a general election in order to qualify for a place on the ballot. It may be voted on at a special election if one is called in the meantime. If adopted by a majority of those voting on the proposition, it becomes effective.

A second method of submitting initiative measures is through a petition to the state legislature signed by 5 percent of the voters. This gives the legislature an opportunity to enact the measure without referring it to the people, or to submit a counterproposal. If the legislature does not enact the proposed law without change, it must be submitted to the voters. Although it requires fewer signers, this procedure has been used only four times and only once was the proposed legislation adopted. The California Constitution Revision Commission recommended in 1966 that this method be repealed.

Acts of the legislature do not go into effect until 30 days after adjournment, during which period 5 percent of the voters may by petition suspend an act pending a referendum vote. Revenue laws, appropriations, acts calling elections, and emergency measures passed by a two-thirds vote of the legislature are not subject to the referendum. Constitutional amendments and bond issues are required by the state constitution to be submitted to a referendum vote. Constitutional amendments and legislative measures proposed by the initiative must relate to one subject only, and it is no longer permissible to designate individuals to hold public office, as was done in the welfare amendment adopted in 1948.

Before each election at which initiative and referendum

proposals are to be voted on, a voters' pamphlet is published by the state and distributed to all voters. This pamphlet contains not only the text and a summary of each measure, but also arguments pro and contra. The arguments for proposed measures are usually prepared by its sponsors; the opposing arguments are prepared by those submitting a referendum petition requiring a vote, or by members of the legislature who are opposed to the measure. If no arguments are submitted, the secretary of state may invite arguments to be submitted for this purpose.

Currently 468,259 qualified signers are required to put an initiative measure on the ballot. Allowing for invalid signatures, a total of about 700,000 must be secured. To secure this number of valid signatures is a formidable undertaking. All petitions are required to be checked by the county registration officers, and only those of registered voters are counted.

Petitions today are almost invariably circulated by paid personnel, and the cost of securing the required number of qualified signers is estimated at $250,000. Several commercial firms in Los Angeles and San Francisco specialize in circulating petitions, and for a fee will deliver the required number of signatures. Most voters sign such petitions with little regard to whether they favor the proposed measure. In one instance the same firm circulated petitions for opposing measures, placing both on the ballot.

Organized labor, employers, churches, farmers, public employees, teachers, organized prohibitionists, realtors, theater owners, liquor interests, commercial fishermen, ship owners, and the oil industry are some of the groups which have proposed legislation through initiative measures. Sometimes the proposed measures have been adopted, but more often they have been defeated.

When initiative and referendum measures are hotly contested, huge publicity campaigns, including the use of newspaper advertisements throughout the state, billboard advertisements, radio and television appeals, and other forms of mass communication are utilized. A number of public-relations firms specialize in handling campaigns for or against such measures. Huge sums of money are spent on controversial measures. According to the reports filed with the secretary of state, an unsuccessful measure in 1958 designed to tax private schools cost the proponents and opponents $1,812,452, and in the same election the expenditures in connection with the so-called "right-to-work" law totaled $3,513,588 ($957,551 by the proponents and $2,556,037 by the opponents). One of the costliest campaigns ever waged was over the "Oil and Gas Conservation Act" in 1956, when the two rival combinations of oil interests spent an officially reported total of $4,874,000 ($3,450,000 by the proponents and $1,424,000 by the opponents), not counting an estimated $2,000,000 in so-called "educational campaigns" before this initiative proposition was drawn up! The proponents and opponents of the proposition on railroad train crews in 1964 reported expenditures of more than $2,400,000.

Usually the side with the most money and the best publicity campaign wins, though not always. In several instances, well-financed campaigns have won through flagrant misrepresentations of the issues. When the motor-bus interests submitted a special tax measure to the voters of the state, the billboard favoring the measure contained a giant picture of a hog, with the slogan: "Drive the hog from the road." The people thought the measure had something to do with roadhogs and voted yes.

How much do the voters know about the measures which appear on the ballot? Obviously no definite answer can be given to this question. It appears that most voters rely upon the recommendations of the newspapers which they read, or those of some other organization, such as chambers of commerce or organized labor. On most propositions little publicity is given in the press, for public interest tends to be centered on the more controversial ballot measures. To become adequately informed on the 20 or more ballot propositions would require much time and study on the part of the voter, which is hardly to be expected. Yet many voters make a serious effort to vote intelligently.

By far the largest use of the initiative and referendum has been to amend the state constitution. Of the 578 initiative measures submitted to popular vote from 1912 until 1964, 477 were constitutional amendments and 101 were legislative proposals and bond issues. The legislature submitted 394 constitutional amendments, of which 238 passed, while 83 constitutional amendments were proposed by initiative, of which 23 were adopted. Of the 57 legislative measures proposed by initiative, only 16 were adopted. Of the 34 acts of the legislature submitted to a referendum vote, 13 were approved and 21 rejected.

Although the initiative and referendum were regarded by many persons as dangerous and radical devices in 1911, the actual practice has not borne out these fears. Numerous radical proposals have been submitted to popular vote, but have almost invariably been voted down. The single-tax plan has been voted down five times. Many pieces of constructive legislation, such as permanent registration of voters, civil-service reform, and the executive budget, have been adopted through initiative measures.

During its early history the initiative was used primarily by groups interested in moral reforms. Prohibition measures appeared on the ballot a number of times; other measures dealt with such subjects as prize fighting, vivisection, compulsory vaccination, and the reading of the Bible in the public schools. Radical economic-reform measures which caused much criticism of the initiative were uncommon before 1930. Conservative interests have also found that they could use the initiative process and on several occasions have secured the adoption of desired legislation which was turned down by the state legislature.

The initiative and referendum, when they were adopted in 1911 as a Progressive reform to counter the power wielded in the state legislature by special-interest groups, provided a "gun behind the door" which the people could use to reject unpopular laws or to enact desired legislation that the legislature had failed to pass. These means of direct legislation made the legislature more responsive to the public interest and provided the voters with the means of passing directly upon important legislation. They were better suited to cope with the problems of the state fifty years ago, when it had a population of less than three million, than they are today. In recent years the use of the initiative and referendum has fundamentally changed. The referendum by petition has virtually lapsed into disuse, and because of the high costs involved, the use of the initiative has greatly declined and today is used almost exclusively by special-interest groups to secure legislation of special benefit to them. During the ten-year period ending in 1964, only 11 initiative measures were submitted to the voters, and only three of these were adopted, two of which were subsequently held unconstitutional by the California Supreme Court. During the same period the legislature submitted 75 constitutional amendments, of which 48 were adopted, and 12 bond issues and other measures, of which 9 were adopted.

In 1911 only about 30,000 signatures were required to place an initiative measure on the ballot; these could be secured with little or no expense by any substantial group of citizens; today an initiative measure requires nearly 500,000 valid signatures, approximately $250,000 to pay for the collection of the signatures, and a minimum of a half million dollars to conduct a publicity campaign. Only organizations or groups which have large financial resources at their disposal are able today to make use of the initiative process. Interest groups sponsoring initiative measures invariably engage a professional public-relations firm to conduct a statewide publicity campaign in which catchy slogans and often misleading propaganda are used to win the approval of the voters. In this way interest groups are able to secure the adoption of legislation granting special benefits or privileges which no legislature would enact. Unless other groups are able and willing to raise a comparable sum of money to oppose such initiative measures, they are likely to be adopted by the voters.

In 1964 the organized realtors placed on the ballot a proposition to prohibit legislation against discrimination in the sale or rental of housing, which a large majority of voters adopted. Theater owners, fearing the threat of competition, placed on the ballot an initiative outlawing the legitimate business of pay television, which the voters, deluged by a campaign urging them to vote for "free" television, approved. Both measures were subsequently declared to be unconstitutional by the state Supreme Court. A third initiative to give an exclusive franchise to a private corporation to run a lottery was fortunately rejected by the voters. Caspar Weinberger, a former member of the Assembly and former Republican state chairman, declared that it is inconceivable that any legislature would have enacted either of these three initiative measures.

Various reforms have been proposed to curb the use of initiatives by special-interest groups to secure legislation for their benefit. In his message to the legislature in 1965, Governor Brown stated: "In recent years [the initiative] has often been used to turn the ballot into a field for jousting among public-relations men wearing the colors of special interests. . . . I believe legislation is needed to prevent special interest from turning the initiative to private gain through the use of professional petition circulators and large sums of money."

The California Constitution Revision Commission in 1965 considered but rejected several proposals to require increased majorities to pass initiative measures, but did recommend that the number of signatures required for statutory initiatives be reduced from 8 to 5 percent of the number of votes cast for governor at the preceding election. This change, if adopted by the voters, will not curb the use of the initiative by interest groups; indeed, it may increase the use by reducing the cost. A more desirable reform would be to require sponsors to submit proposed initiative measures to the legislature for its consideration during a specified period before petitions are circulated to secure the required number of signatures. This procedure would give advance notice of a proposed initiative and subject it to public scrutiny by the press and interested organizations; it would also enable the legislature to conduct an inquiry into the need and probable effects of such legislation. It would undoubtedly curb the use of the initiative process by special-interest groups for their own benefit and would reduce the necessity for expensive campaigns to defeat proposals that are contrary to the public interest.

THE RECALL OF PUBLIC OFFICERS

Every elective officer in California, including judges, is subject to removal by the voters at a recall election. A petition to recall a state officer must be signed by 12 percent of the number of qualified voters who cast ballots at the election when the officer was elected. It must be circulated in at least five counties and be signed by at least 1 percent of the voters in each of five counties. If the official is elected from a single county, the recall petition must be signed by at least 20 percent of the qualified voters of that county.

County, city, and other local officers may be recalled under similar provisions, except that before the circulation of a petition to recall a city officer, charges must be published and the officer given 14 days to answer such charges. In a recall election, a majority of the voters voting at the election determine whether the incumbent is to be recalled or to retain his office. At the same election the voters also vote for a candidate to succeed to the office, should the incumbent be recalled.

The recall of public officers differs very significantly in one respect from the initiative and referendum, namely, it is rarely used. There have been few instances in which a public official has been recalled while in office. A mayor of Los Angeles was recalled in 1938 following sensational charges of corruption, but more recent attempts to recall the mayors of San Francisco and Los Angeles failed. In 1950 an election to recall three members of the Oakland city council who had voted for public housing was held, the recall fight being led by opponents of public housing, but only one of the three councilmen was recalled. In 1961 the mayor of Albany, who had been a highly controversial personality in local politics, was recalled in a special election.

chapter 5

On Being Active in Politics

☆

Not every citizen can run for public office or serve on the local school board, city council, or in the state legislature. Not every citizen can become an active party worker. But every citizen can and should become informed about politics—national, state, and local—and exercise the duties of citizenship with intelligence and zeal. The function of the politician, including those who serve in public office, is an essential one in modern society. Instead of being looked down upon, politics should be regarded as a worthy avocation, if not vocation, one which should attract the ablest and finest of our citizens. It requires much time and effort and involves many heartaches and disappointments, but the rewards are often highly gratifying. If one is civic-spirited and desires an opportunity to render conspicuous public service, to participate in the important decisions in his community, to make it a better place to live, and to gain the honor, prestige, and recognition for such service, he can do no better than to enter a political career. But he must first prepare himself by an internship of active work and participation in civic and political affairs.

It is the duty of every citizen not only to register and vote, but also to do so with intelligence on the basis of an informed judgment. Unless he can vote intelligently, it is better not to vote at all. But the duties of citizenship do not stop with voting. The good citizen obeys the law, earns a living, pays his taxes, renders other services required of him, and is a good neighbor. In a democracy he has another important function to perform—to participate in the formation of public opinion. This requires him to keep abreast of the times and to become informed on the major public issues. Obviously, he cannot become an expert on all subjects and must select those of greatest concern to him or those on which he is best equipped to make a contribution. An informed, intelligent, and vigilant public opinion is a prime requisite to democratic government.

In the past, educated and patriotic citizens have often remained aloof from politics and political parties, partly because they regarded politics as dirty business, and partly because they prided themselves on being independent of partisanship. This attitude is mistaken and unfortunate. The highest form of citizenship is exercised by the person who joins a party and works actively to make it better and more effective. America's genius for government, on which our future depends, requires the best, not the second best, to enter politics. The rewards in human satisfactions are often greater than for any other line of endeavor. The citizen who is an active party worker, who is an officer in a political club, or who serves on the school board or city council or in some other capacity, is rewarded not in money but in new friendships, in added opportunities for service, and in the recognition and prestige which he earns.

How does one start? Take an active interest in community, state, and national affairs. Keep well read on public affairs. Attend public meetings. Have an opinion on local issues, but be sure of your facts first. Join a political club. Become acquainted with local political leaders and volunteer your services. Within a short time they will be in demand, and you will be started on a political career.

Usually it is necessary for the beginner to start at the bottom, to ring doorbells and make himself useful. He should be prepared for the realities of politics. Not all political workers are idealists, and not all will have the same goals; some will be in politics for what they think they can get out of it. Not all persons who are political leaders start at the bottom. Richard Nixon and John Kennedy did not enter political careers by ringing doorbells. Political parties need persons who have achieved distinction in other walks of life to enter politics at a high level.

Persons who plan to enter politics as a public career should first acquire standing in their community, and a livelihood! Politics and the law are the most frequent combination, but businessmen, labor leaders, members of the professions, and housewives should also be more widely represented. If you wish to prepare yourself for a public career or merely want to take an active part in politics and public affairs, join local civic organizations and take an active part. Develop a lively interest in community problems and serve on advisory committees. Become thoroughly informed about such problems as housing, city planning, schools, welfare, recreation, juvenile delinquency, and interracial relations, and participate in their solution. If you enjoy community service and the human contacts which it affords, you have the makings of a good politician.

Suggested Readings
on California Politics

☆

Alexander, Herbert E., and Laura L. Denny. *Regulation of Political Finance*. Berkeley: Institute of Governmental Studies, University of California, 1966.

Allen, Don A., Sr. *Legislative Sourcebook: The California Legislature and Reapportionment*. Published by the California Assembly, Sacramento: State Printing Office, 1965.

Bean, Walton. *Boss Ruef's San Francisco*. Berkeley: University of California Press, 1952.

Buchanan, William. *Legislative Partisanship: The Deviant Case of California*. Berkeley: University of California Press, 1963.

Burke, Robert E. *Olson's New Deal for California*. Berkeley and Los Angeles: University of California Press, 1953.

California Election Laws, 1966. Published by A. Carlisle and Co., San Francisco. Available from county clerk or registrar of voters.

California League of Women Voters. *California Voters' Handbook*. Pasadena, 1964.

Carney, Francis. *The Rise of the Democratic Clubs in California*. New York: Henry Holt and Company, 1958.

Cresap, Dean R. *Party Politics in the Golden State*. Los Angeles: The Haynes Foundation, 1954.

Crouch, Winston W. *The Initiative and Referendum in California*. Los Angeles: The Haynes Foundation, 1950.

Crouch, Winston W., Dean E. McHenry, John C. Bollens, and Stanley Scott. *California Government and Politics*. 3rd ed., Englewood Cliffs, New Jersey: Prentice-Hall, 1964.

Farelly, David, and Ivan Hinderaker. *The Politics of California*. New York: Ronald Press, 1951.

Hyink, Bernard L., Seyom Brown, and Ernest W. Thacker. *Politics and Government in California*. 4th ed., New York: Thomas Y. Crowell Co., 1965.

Lee, Eugene C. *California Votes, 1928–1960*. Berkeley: Institute of Governmental Studies, University of California, 1963.

Lee, Eugene C. *The Politics of Nonpartisanship*. Berkeley: University of California Press, 1960.

McWilliams, Carey. *California: The Great Exception*. New York: A. A. Wyn, 1949.

Mowry, George E. *The California Progressives*. Berkeley: University of California Press, 1951.

Turner, Henry A., and John A. Vieg. *The Government and Politics of California*. 2nd ed., New York: McGraw-Hill Book Co., 1964.

Wilson, James Q. *The Amateur Democrat*. Chicago: University of Chicago Press, 1962.

Index

☆

AFL-CIO apportionment plan, 104, 106

Alexander, Herbert E., 68n

Allen, Don A., Sr., 103n

Americans for Democratic Action, 48

Anderson, Glenn M., 31

Anderson, Totton J., 15n, 19n, 22n, 23n, 112n

Assembly districts, 1965 (fig.), 96

Baus and Ross Company, 66

Bean, Walton, 5n

Beek, Joseph, 91

Birch, John, Society, 17, 21, 23, 29

Bonelli, Frank G., 105

Brown, Edmund G., 13, 19, 27–31, 63, 67, 68

Bryce, James G., 2

California Democratic Council, 39, 48, 51–53, 64

California politics, pattern of, 37–39

California Republican Assembly, 15, 39, 48–51

Campaign expenditures, 19, 68–75, 84, 116–118

Campaign tactics, 64–68

Christopher, George, 21, 26, 30

Communist party, 42

Congressional districts, 1961 (fig.), 93

Constitution Revision Commission, 119

County central committee, 44–46

Cranston, Alan, 69–71

Creel, George, 10

Cresap, Dean R., 83n

Cross filing, 36

Crouch, Winston W., 113n

David, Paul A., 102n

Democratic Associates, 48

Democratic clubs: See California Democratic Council

Democratic party, 32–37, 64
  See also Political parties
Denny, Laura L., 68*n*
Dickson, Edward A., 3, 5
Direct primary, 57–81

Eisenberg, Ralph, 102*n*
Elections:
  1962, 14–19
  1964, 19–24
  1966, 25–32
  campaign tactics, 64–68
  nonpartisan, 56, 77–81
  types, 55–56
EPIC movement, 9–10

Fair Campaign Practices Committee, 67
Filing fees, 61

Gerrymander, 110–112
Goldwater, Barry J., 19–22, 62, 63

Haynes, John R., 3
Heard, Alexander, 68*n*
Heney, Francis J., 5
Herrin, William F., 3

Initiative and referendum, 39, 112–120

Johnson, Hiram, 5, 8
Judges, election of, 76

Kennedy, John F., 75
Knight, Goodwin J., 13, 16
Knowland, William F., 13, 14, 20
Kuchel, Thomas, 16, 21

Lane, Robert E., 78*n*
Leary, Mary Ellen, 108*n*
Lee, Eugene C., 15*n*, 19*n*, 22*n*, 23*n*, 79, 112*n*

Legislative apportionment:
  Assembly districts, 1965 (*fig.*), 96
  California Supreme Court decision, 95–98
  comparison of 1961 and 1965 Senate apportionments, 99–100
  congressional districts, 1961 (*fig.*), 93
  history of, 100–108
  probable effects of 1965 Senate apportionment, 108–110
  senatorial districts, 1965 (*fig.*), 97
  U.S. Supreme Court decision, 94–95
Legislature, politics of the, 90–94
Lerner, Harry, and Associates, 66
Lincoln, Luther H., 92
Lincoln-Roosevelt League, 6
Lobbies, 84–88
Los Angeles Times, 6
Lynch, Thomas C., 31

Martin, Joseph W., 50
Merriam, Frank, 10
Mowry, George E., 3*n*

National Federation of Republican Women, 48
National party committee, 44
Newspapers, 88–89
Nixon, Richard M., 13–19, 68
Nominating conventions, 58
Nominations, 57–64
Nonpartisan elections, 56, 77–81
Nonpartisanship, 47, 76–80

Official party organization (*fig.*), 42

Olson, Culbert L., 11

Parkinson, Gaylord B., 25
Phelan, James D., 9
Platforms, party, 43
Political parties:
  county central committee, 44–46
  national committee, 44
  official party organization (fig.),
    42
  qualification of, 41
  registration trends, 9, 32–37
  state central committee, 43–44
  state convention, 42–43
  unofficial political organizations,
    39, 46–53
Preprimary endorsements, 59–61
Presidential preference primary,
  19–22, 61–64
Press, 88–89
Pressure groups, 83–88
Primary, direct, 57–81
Pro-America, 48
Progressive movement, 2–8
Progressive party, 7–9
Prohibition party, 41
Public-relations firms, 65, 66

Reagan, Ronald, 25–31
Reapportionment: See Legislative
  apportionment
Recall of public officers, 120
Registration of voters, 56–57
  1932–1966 (table), 33
Republican Associates of Los An-
  geles, 48
Republican era, 9
Republican party, 32–37, 64
  See also Political parties
Reynolds v. Sims, 94–95

Robinson, Joseph A., Associates,
  66
Roosevelt, Theodore, 7, 75
Rowell, Chester, 2, 6
Ruef, Abe, 4

Safe legislative districts, 24
Salinger, Pierre, 69–70
Samish, Arthur, 83, 87
San Francisco Chronicle, 29, 50
Senatorial districts, 1965 (fig.), 97
Shell, Joseph C., 16
Silliman, James W., 92
Sinclair, Upton, 9–10
Southern Pacific Railroad, 3–8, 110
Speaker of the Assembly, 92–94
State central committee, 43–44
State convention, 42–43
Suffrage qualifications, 56

Television in political campaigns,
  70

Union Labor party, 4
United Republicans of California,
  22, 48
Unofficial political organizations,
  39, 46–53
Unruh, Jesse, 14, 31, 106

Velie, Lester, 83
Vote for President in California,
  1932–1964 (table), 34
Voting qualifications, 56–57

Warren, Earl, 10–13, 65, 94
Weinberger, Caspar, 22, 119
Whitaker and Baxter, 66
Workingman's party, 2

Yorty, Samuel, 27, 64
Young Democrats, 48
Young Republicans, 48